The Senior High School Principalship

Volume III: The Summary Report

Lloyd E. McCleary

Scott D. Thomson

National Association of Secondary School Principals
1904 Association Drive • Reston, Virginia 22091

About the authors:

Lloyd E. McCleary is professor of educational administration, Graduate School of Education, University of Utah. Scott D. Thomson is Deputy Executive Director, National Association of Secondary School Principals.

ISBN 0-88210-098-X
Copyright © 1979
All Rights Reserved
National Association of Secondary School Principals
1904 Association Drive, Reston, Va. 22091

V.3

Contents

**Steering Committee
for the
Study of the Senior High School Principalship**

Lloyd E. McCleary
Richard A. Gorton
Judith S. Greene
Brother Eagan Hunter
Henry L. Miller
Eugene R. Smoley
Scott D. Thomson, *Chairman*

Research Team for the Study

Lloyd E. McCleary, *Chairman*
Richard A. Gorton
Kenneth E. McIntyre
David R. Byrne
Scott D. Thomson

Supported by the Rockefeller Family Fund

Foreword

THE PRINCIPALSHIP DEFINITELY has changed during the past decade in response to the many forces acting upon high schools in the late 1960s and early 1970s. Certainly the emergence of professional negotiations, of court decisions on student affairs and on desegregation, and the constantly shifting priorities of the public for schools presages a different principalship in the late 1970s than existed in the mid 1960s.

Considering these circumstances and the fact that the principal is the key to a good school, NASSP decided that high priority must be given to a national study of the principalship so that the current nature of the assignment as well as the background and training of principals could be determined. Consequently, a steering committee was formed under the chairmanship of Deputy Executive Director Scott Thomson to launch the study.

Supporting funds were pledged by the Rockefeller Family Fund and the research team went to work. The steering committee and research team agreed that the study should consist of three parts: a random sample survey of 1,600 principals, an in-depth interview with 60 "effective" principals, and a look at future forces and conditions acting upon the principalship. This publication, Volume III, summarizes the first two volumes, reports on future forces and conditions likely to affect the high school principalship, describes the private and religious school principal, and profiles the principalship of the future.

A special note of thanks goes to respondents of the three questionnaires which form the data base for the complete study, to Lloyd McCleary as leader of the research team, and to members of the steering committee.

We believe this summary volume provides an incisive, comprehensive capstone to NASSP's national study of the high school principalship.

Owen B. Kiernan
Executive Director
NASSP

Introduction

WHEN THE NASSP STEERING COMMITTEE for the national high school principals' study finalized its plans, three research reports were projected. The first was to be a report of a national survey of a randomly selected sample of senior high school principals. The second was to be a report of an in-depth examination of 60 senior high principals judged to be effective. The third, represented by this volume, was to be a synthesis of the results of the first two studies and to include projections into the future.

The futures commentary was to be derived from data of the first two studies plus a survey of educational issues and conditions as seen by policy makers who have the perspectives from which to make reliable judgments. Surprisingly perhaps, the plans materialized as projected—largely due to the cooperation of the large number of principals and citizens who participated together with concentrated work by the steering committee and the research team.

Volumes I and II contain the findings of the survey study and the study of principals judged to be effective. Data and findings along with detailed descriptions of the methodology and instruments are provided elsewhere and are not treated here. Note should be taken, however, that the survey was correlated with the NASSP survey published in 1965 so that a number of useful comparisons were possible. Thus, a longitudinal perspective was obtained using the 1965 data as a base line. Further, the interview schedules employed in the study of effective principals were interrelated with the survey questionnaire. In this way data of the random sample survey could be compared with interview responses. Also, the survey provides normative-descriptive data which can be used to obtain insight into factors that distinguish effective principals from a random selection.

The amount and "richness" of the data have permitted the research staff to go well beyond the original expectations for Volume III. During the course of data analysis it was found that sufficient grounds existed to carry out several additional investigations. The nonpublic school principals (religious, religious affiliated, private) comprised an independent subsample which revealed characteristics different from the total group of principals. Questions about similarities and differences of the effective principals and the random sample and the comparability of interview and survey data indicated the need to obtain survey data from the 60 effective principals. The nature and amount of the data about administrative tasks and about decision making-problem solving was such that more intensive examination of these two areas was undertaken. These four areas were separately attacked by four members of the research staff and their findings were made available to the authors for use in Volume III.

PREPARATION OF THIS REPORT

Volume III is not a research report in the usual sense; rather, it is a commentary or examination in essay style of the total study—encompassing the 1977 survey, the study of effective principals, the futures study, the 1965 survey data, and the four ancillary studies noted above. It brings together the findings and speculates about them in terms of the principal and the principalship today and the directions in which change is likely to occur in the future. Data, as such, are not presented except as illustrative, and the reader is encouraged to refer to Volumes I and II and to the studies which are noted at the end of this report.

The preparation of this report represents a serious effort to examine the findings and reevaluate the data of separate but carefully interrelated studies. A number of questions were kept constantly in mind by the writers and may serve to guide the reader in making his own judgments about the presentation:

- How stable are the perceptions of principals and "significant others"; would these perceptions change considerably over a relatively short time span?

- If a different group were selected, would the results be different?

- Assuming that these data represent the true state of affairs, what effects would traumatic events have on conditions reported; events such as a major tax revolt, energy crisis, serious recession, etc.?

- Which changes now in evidence will phase out, which will persist?

Obviously, there are no simple answers, nor are there absolute assurances. These questions are offered as illustrative of those which concerned the writers. We do know that the group of principals studied survived and even thrived on the turmoil of the sixties, the energy crisis of the seventies, and several equally traumatic events. We do know that the data, where they could be verified by cross checking, were reliable and accurate. We do know that the principals as a group are relatively stable—not only in point of view and emotion but even in tenure in their districts. We think the results can be trusted, and we offer them for the reader's examination and critical appraisal. We believe this volume will be useful as a benchmark or a reference for the reader's own thinking.

THE ORGANIZATION OF THIS REPORT

This report begins with a selection and presentation of the central findings of the national random sample survey and of the effective principals study. These two studies and the separate investigations derived from the data provide a profile of the high school principal today.

The nonpublic school principal is then treated in Chapter III because of the significant differences found between the nonpublic school principal and his colleagues in public schools.

Finally, two aspects of the future are drawn for analysis: future forces and conditions, and the future principalship. Each is treated in the final chapters of this volume.

1

Significant Findings from the National Survey

THE FIRST PHASE OF THE COMPLETE STUDY of the senior high school principal was a random sample survey. The survey questionnaire was composed of 184 questions, arranged as 66 items, requiring 375 independent responses. Of the 184 questions, 123 were replications from an NASSP survey published in 1965. The earlier study and the questions used from it permit comparisons between conditions in 1965 and 1977.

The 1977 questionnaire was sent to 1,600 randomly selected senior high school principals and 1,131 usable responses were received within the specified time limit, a return of 70.6 percent. These questionnaires form the basis of the study, along with the 1965 data reported in Volume I, and are the original source of findings treated in this chapter. In addition, the writers referred to the ancillary studies (as noted in the Foreword) dealing with tasks and problem-solving behavior, the survey questionnaires completed by the group of effective principals, and other current related literature.

This chapter first treats the principal as a person and includes belief patterns, training, and experience. Commentary then turns to the job itself, to the school, and the community setting. As indicated, this is not a summary of the findings of the national survey—these are already provided in Volume I. Rather, from the basic perceptions of principals an attempt is made to highlight significant findings and to provide a perspective to deal with interpretations and implications.

The Principal as a Professional Person   5

The principal occupies the key position in school organization; he is not a passive or neutral administrative officer. The school is a social system with belief patterns, authority structures, formal and informal communications systems, special interest groups, etc.; and the influence of the principal reaches into each of these elements. The principal brings to the school a unique background of training, experience, professional beliefs and attitudes which condition his approach to what and how he attempts to influence.

Persons who become principals are predisposed to the position by past experiences, particularly in educational institutions, and by association with others in the educational enterprise. They follow certain career routes and training patterns. Because of these experiences they take on particular belief patterns, career aspirations, and a particular identity with their colleagues. The question of how diverse principals as a group actually are becomes basic to a consideration of personal-professional characteristics. The national survey data provide some interesting and surprising insights about these characteristics.

Senior high school principals of the late 1970s are different as a group from principals of the early 1960s. Their median age is slightly older, but as a group there are significantly fewer younger (under age 40) principals and significantly fewer older (over age 55) principals. They assume their first principalship at a later age (after 35) than formerly, and they have completed more formal education, including the master's degree plus additional work or the specialist and doctoral degrees: 85 percent of all senior high school principals are in one of these categories versus only 56 percent in 1965. They remain predominantly white/male: seven percent are female; four percent give ethnic origin as nonwhite.

The one external condition which undoubtedly had a dramatic impact upon the nation's principals was the pervasive social turmoil of the late sixties and early seventies. Direct evidence is not available, but one could speculate that the age of the first principalship, the decrease in older principals, and the low percentage of female principals might be attributed to this condition. The increased size of secondary schools, the many new services causing organizational complexity, a string of legislative mandates, the declining enrollments, and teacher militancy certainly are contributing factors to the changing principalship and are considered later in this chapter.

Belief Patterns of Principals

One of the more dramatic changes found in the personal/professional characteristics of principals is a shift in what might be termed the "belief patterns" of principals. Twenty broad educational issues over a wide range of topics were presented to the principals who were asked to indicate their degree of agreement or disagreement. The statements dealt with such issues as: compulsory education, court decisions, aid to private and religious schools, student rights, ability grouping, limitation of political discussion in the classroom, and emphasis upon academic work. Fourteen of these statements of basic beliefs were repeated from the 1965 study. In *each* of the 14 statements a shift in attitude was of such magnitude that a Harris or Gallup poll would use terms like "radical" or "fundamental" to describe them. Statistical tests of each item indicated significance above the .01 level with most above the .001 level.

The most dramatic shifts, representing reversals of professional opinion between 1965 to 1977, found principals in 1977 *agreeing* with these statements:

- Hostile or disinterested youth should not be required to attend school;
- Schools require too little academic work;
- Schools should provide specific job training;
- Schools should develop special programs for the talented; and
- Schools are not producing enough scholars in the fields of human needs, energy, environment, medicine.

A sixth reversal but in the direction of *disagreement* with the statement (agreed with by principals in 1965) is that court decisions concerning racial segregation are correct as they apply to public schools.

Principals in 1977 more strongly *agreed* than did principals in 1965 with statements that the principle of universal secondary education is essential to American society. They *agreed* but less strongly with the statement that grouping by IQ or achievement was desirable in academic subjects. They *disagreed,* as did principals in 1965, but much less strongly with statements that:

- Federal aid be made available to private and religious schools;
- Court decisions concerning prayer and bible reading are correct; and
- Limitations should be placed on political discussions in the classroom.

These items, although showing a similar direction of agreement or disagreement, are items upon which a significant shift occurred between 1965 and 1977. Continued shifts could lead to a reversal of position as occurred with the other issues.

The 14 items, all showing significant shifts, together with the six additional items presented to principals only in the 1977 study, indicate that principals do think deeply about broad educational issues, that they tend to hold similar opinions as a professional group, and that these opinions do change with time. In an era of many views, it is interesting that principals are in relative agreement among themselves. Only in two instances, (1) court decisions concerning prayer and bible reading (48 percent agree, 52 percent disagree) and (2) racial segregation (49 percent agree, 51 percent disagree), was there a close division of opinion.

Another aspect of the basic beliefs of principals involves their views about educational priorities for high schools. If the principals' views of educational issues have changed dramatically, what of their views of the priorities for the educational program? As unexpected as the changes noted previously about educational issues is the relative *stability* of priorities for secondary education. Eleven statements of educational tasks were presented to principals for ranking; eight were used in the 1965 study and these were repeated in 1977 exactly as stated earlier. The rank order of priorities was *identical* for the eight repeated items with only two exceptions. The statement dealing with development of positive self-concept shifted from seventh place in 1965 to second place in 1977, and development of moral and spiritual values shifted from second place to fourth place. Two items that were presented to principals only in the 1977 study, "career planning and occupational training" and "preparation for family life," were ranked fifth and sixth. The educational task ranked first in 1965 and again in 1977 was "acquisition of basic skills" followed in the same relative rank order except as noted above by "development of critical inquiry and problem solving," "understanding the American political, economic, and social system," and "preparation for a changing world."

The relative stability of educational priorities is of interest especially because of the dramatic shifts in beliefs relative to broad educational issues. Principals in 1977 view the educational program as seeking its goals in about the same priority order as did principals in 1965 although today's principals see the institutional contexts for providing this education as needing to be significantly different.

Preparation of Principals

The formal educational levels achieved by principals was mentioned in the opening section of this chapter. The principal today is much better prepared academically than was the principal of the mid-1960s. Furthermore, the emphasis of that preparation in terms of undergraduate majors has changed, as have preferences for graduate preparation.

The range of undergraduate majors of those entering the principalship has always been diverse with no one undergraduate field dominating. The academic disciplines of humanities, sciences, and social sciences combined, represent the content fields of about two-thirds of the undergraduate majors. Within this group, however, the number of social science majors almost doubled between 1965 and 1977. This may reflect the concern for social conditions in society and schools.

Whether educational administration would be further strengthened by having its practitioners arrive through a common undergraduate preparation as in medicine (biological sciences) or engineering (physical sciences) remains a moot question. At the graduate level the major field of study for principals is dominated by the study of educational administration, over 70 percent, and when combined with other fields of education, includes more than 85 percent of current principals.

Within the field of educational administration dramatic shifts have occurred in course work emphasis. These shifts are indicated by principals' ratings of the courses they considered essential to success. In 1977, school law, curriculum and program development, management, supervision of instruction, and human relations were all rated essential (in the order given) by more than 70 percent of the principals surveyed. In 1965, only one course, supervision of instruction, was rated essential to success by more than 50 percent of the principals.

Career Routes and Career Aspirations

A significant change has occurred in the career routes to the high school principalship. These changes represent patterns which are not likely to be reversed because they stem from conditions that require increased preparation, longer periods of experience, and requirements of intimate knowledge of the community and the school. Almost all current high school principals appointed since 1965 had experience as assistant high school principals or as middle school principals or assistant principals—or some combination of these. In 1965 the high school principal was more likely to have been a guidance counselor (48 percent) or an elementary principal (38 percent), but not so today. Furthermore, tenure both in the initial administrative post and in the principalship is longer—63 percent of the principals today reported being in their current post more than four years.

Whether the high school principalship has been, or will become, an acceptable, recognized, and satisfactory capstone career post is not clearly established. It is known that principals are relatively satisfied in 1977 with their jobs; they see the role as stimulating, rewarding, and adequate in prestige and autonomy as contrasted to the 1965 study and other previous studies. However, they also report the job as more demanding, more time consuming, and more conflict ridden than in the past. How these conditions reflect upon career aspirations and mobility can only be determined in a limited way. More principals (33 percent vs. 14 percent) now aspire to a superintendency or central office position, yet fewer indicate that they seek other types of positions. None indicated in 1977 that they would seek a principalship in a smaller school or make a lateral move to a comparable school.

9

SUMMARY

The 1977 national survey, serving as a data base, provides a view of the high school principal as a professional person that in many ways was not anticipated. It presents a surprising, but definitely not a discouraging picture. The principal today is more mature, better prepared, and more satisfied with the role of principal than was his predecessor. The high school principal enjoys job stability and security, but he is still a mobile person. There exists today much more uniformity in preparation and career routes, yet there is still diversity;

the role is not a closed one. The contemporary principal exhibits a view of broad educational issues that appears to reflect current social and political conditions. He sees the central tasks of education to be relatively stable but he recognizes the institutional arrangements as changing along with society. These two views are not in conflict and probably represent a healthy stance for the leadership of the nation's schools. Furthermore there appears to be solid agreement within the principals' group about these views.

The Principal's Job and the High School

The high school today is a much different institution than existed in the mid-1960s. Regardless of the cliche that schools haven't changed in 50 years, secondary schools have matured and apparently are thriving. The impact of the "mass culture," the cosmopolitanism of the community and the students, the demands of the mobile-technological society—all have caused an impact. The schools, comprised of those who learn in them, teach in them, administer them, and support them, appear to have responded reasonably well to rapid and often traumatic changes.

The public comprehensive high school still dominates the educational scene (over 82 percent); parochial and private/religious affiliated schools remain about the same in relative numbers; while the private school has declined in number (3.0 percent in 1965, 0.9 percent in 1977). The alternative high school made its appearance during this decade and accounts now for 1.4 percent of the total. School size and expenditure levels have increased markedly. Only three percent of the high schools now spend less than $500.00 per pupil per year; in 1965, 76 percent of the high schools spent less than this. In 1965, only 7.0 percent spent more than $700.00 per pupil; today 7.0 percent spend *more* than $2,100 per pupil. The magnitude of increase for the lower expenditure schools is 17 times during this 12-year period.

The median size of the high school today is 1,000-1,500 students, while in 1965 it was less than 500, with 65 percent of all high schools being under 500 enrollment then.

The increase in size and expenditure levels made possible a diversity of programs as evidenced by a major increase in special/categorical programs, alternative programs, introduction of more educational technology, and improved facilities. Some increase in the formal training of teaching staff occurred. The major impact upon administration was new complexities, coordination imperatives, and added responsibilities.

Changes in the principalship also include new time demands, with principals reporting in 1977 more time spent on the job (56 hours per week) together with serious administrative roadblocks such as growing administrative detail, lack of time, and variations in teacher competency coming highest on the list. Apathetic parents and problem students follow as serious roadblocks—these two items did not appear in 1965. With increased time demands coming from larger schools and these other factors, principals teach much less frequently than in the past. Their allocation of time also is not as they would like to have it. They report that most time is spent on management whereas they would prefer that most time be spent on program development. In addition, they spend more time than they would like on student behavior and district office activities. They spend less time than they would like on program development, on planning, and on professional development.

Despite the problems, increased responsibilities and time pressures, principals today feel they have more job security, prestige, independent thought and action, opportunity to help others, and possibilities for self-fulfillment than did principals in the mid-1960s. Furthermore, principals today are more mature (older and more experienced), better trained, and have been tested by the turmoil of the late 1960s and early 1970s. These characteristics along with their larger, more diverse schools means that many are accorded more autonomy, more independent action, and more authority over their schools than in the past. The evidence supports this view.

The principal today is better rewarded than in the mid-1960s in job satisfaction and also in salary. In 1977, 2.0 percent of the principals received less than $12,000 versus 18 percent less than $6,000 ($11,250 in 1977 dollars). At the median range, however, the 1977 principal received $25,600 compared to $15,750 (adjusted to 1977 dollars) for the 1965 principal. Only 10 percent of the principals in 1965 received an adjusted salary level of $24,000 compared to 40 percent of the principals in 1977. How much this apparent increase can be attributed to increased training, responsibility, and work load is debatable. The gains are real ones but, we would argue, not sufficient to offset changed work conditions and the improved preparation and experience needed.

SUMMARY

11

There is no question that the high school today is larger, more complex, more fraught with problems and conflict—and much more demanding of administrators—than in the past. At the same time additional per pupil expenditures, special programs for students, and increased specialization of staff have been provided. Also, the current principal is better trained, more experienced, and better rewarded. He works longer hours under greater stress than in the past, but he does not appear to be overwhelmed by stress. In fact, most principals apparently derive great satisfaction from their jobs. The time demands alone require examination however. One must ask whether a person can perform a satisfactory leadership role as the job is now structured, considering the expectations for time and job tasks that currently exist.

The School Setting

The high school today and its administration is strongly influenced by state requirements, federal regulations, central office/board policies and directives, community agencies, and parents. Principals, rather surprisingly, do not view desegregation as a problem or a constraint. However, they do report Title IX (60 percent) and student rights (62 percent) as federal regulation problems. On the state level, principals see compulsory attendance (58 percent) and categorical fund requirements as troublesome; these were followed by accountability demands and graduation requirements. At the community level, principals identified parental lack of interest (79 percent), parental demands (63 percent), and pressures of special groups (53 percent) as definite constraints.

Most of these concerns represent dilemmas; although most principals see them as constraints and impositions, they also view them as necessary and, in the long run, beneficial. Lack of parental interest represents a different kind of problem. Principals are troubled by it but do not appear to have decided with any consensus about what should be done. One facet of the dilemma is that principals want more parental influence over student behavior but not more direct participation in school affairs. In this matter of parental influence over student behavior, principals feel relatively powerless to alter parent/youth relationships.

Concerning parental participation in school affairs, principals appear to have definite, but often contractory, ideas. Many principals are concerned about interference and tend to limit, and even exclude, parental involvement in program planning, in administrative policy, or other matters directly bearing upon the educational process. Principals often will permit parent participation in these matters as advisory or informational only. Principals generally welcome parent participation in student activities, in fund raising, and in other service and resource functions, but not in decision-making roles. An unresolved question is how principals can expect one kind of participation without the other in an era of college educated clientele and consumerism.

Concerning relationships with the central office and school board, principals are positive about general support levels, ability to communicate needs and problems, and the services offered. They do cite policy restrictions and central office/board interference as two serious constraints. Principals are active in seeking more autonomy and freedom of action; they also are quite sensitive to "being treated alike." As the principal continues to improve his professional status and performance, as he has since the 1965 study, new administrative arrangements will need to be formulated to provide flexibility and yet maintain accountability for each school site.

This chapter represents a view of the principal and the principalship as it exists today. By and large the view is an optimistic one. Much ground has been gained though problems certainly remain. The principalship presented is one of confidence and competence, of reasonable professional unity together with an optimism that problems can be attacked and overcome. The continued viability of the role, as evidenced by time demands and task priorities, requires serious consideration as does the role of the patrons of the high school.

13

2 Significant Findings from the Study of Effective Principals

THE SECOND PHASE OF THE NATIONAL study of the high school principalship involved an in-depth study of 60 "effective" principals. The results are published as Volume II of this series. Information was gathered from principals at their schools using a 25-page structured interview instrument. In addition, a 10-page instrument was used to gather data from four groups of "significant others": teachers, students, parents, and central office/board. Interviews with principals typically lasted three to five hours, while discussions with each group of the "significant others" took about two hours.

The sample for the study included 60 senior high school principals from across the United States located in four population categories: (1) urban, (2) suburban, (3) medium city, and (4) rural. The principals were identified through the use of a reputational-selection process using criteria provided to three nominators in each state: (1) the director of secondary education in the Department of Public Instruction, (2) the executive secretary of the state association of secondary school principals, and (3) an experienced professor of school administration. This process developed a pool of 102 principals nominated by two or more of the above sources. Verifications of excellence were then made by telephone conversations with district superintendents, causing three nominees to be dropped. The final group of 60 subjects was selected to provide balance by geographical region and population classification.

Because the research team wanted to study effective principals from several perspectives, each principal in the sample was asked to identify student, teacher, parent, and central office/board representatives for interviewing according to specified role. For instance, the interviewed teachers included: (1) president of the teachers group in the school, (2) the English chair, (3) the business education chair, and (4) a nontenure teacher. Each of these four referent groups was interviewed separately.

It is important to note that the study did not intend to identify the "one best principal" in each state. Such an identification was considered neither possible nor desirable. The study does identify, however,

15

persons representative of the more effective principals in each state according to the criteria defined by the research team and applied by the nominators.

This chapter addresses first the question of job conditions: responsibilities, priorities, expectations, etc. The strategies and techniques used by effective principals to attack job tasks are then considered, followed by an analysis of personal characteristics, of professional outlook, and of relationships with referent groups. Finally, recommendations for making the principalship a more solidly professional position are outlined.

Job Conditions

Certain conditions of the principalship shape the structure in which a principal must operate. This framework applies regardless of idiosyncratic differences from community to community. Such job factors always are present regardless of the school setting. These continuing conditions include certain areas of responsibility (personnel, management, student behavior, etc.), role expectations, priorities, constraints, resources, and time.

AREAS OF RESPONSIBILITY

The effective principals controlled their job responsibilities well, devoting most time and attention to the three areas they consider to have top priority: (1) personnel, (2) program development, and (3) school management. They did, however, spend more hours on problems of student behavior than they would prefer, ranking it sixth in the way time should be spent but placing it fifth in time actually spent.

Some interesting differences arise between the 60 effective principals and the national random sample of principals concerning the nine areas of responsibility. Both groups were asked the way they *should* spend their time and the way they *do* spend their time. The results are given in Table 1.

While both groups agree about the way time *should* be spent in the task areas, the effective principals are more adroit at actually spending time as planned. The one exception is "district meetings," a requirement which provides little opportunity for personal control. The random sample group appears to fall seriously short of devoting the time they would like in two areas of responsibility: (1) program development, and (2) professional development. They also spend considerably more time than they would like with problems of student behavior.

These findings indicate that effectiveness, as it relates to job responsibilities, may not be so much a matter of knowing *what* is important as of knowing *how* to actually control time for use upon tasks judged as most essential. This means, in part, not getting tied up in resolving student misbehavior to the detriment of program development and professional growth.

16

TABLE 1
Time Allocation

Should Spend Time			Do Spend Time	
Effectives	Random	Area of Responsibility	Effectives	Random
1	1	Program Development (curriculum, instructional leadership)	3	5
2	2	Personnel (evaluation, advising, conferencing, recruiting)	2	2
3	3	School Management (weekly calendar, office, budget, correspondence, memos, etc.)	1	1
5	4	Student Activities (meetings, supervision, planning)	4	3
6	7	Student Behavior (discipline, attendance, meetings)	5	4
8	8	Community (PTA, advisory groups, parent conferences, etc.)	8	8
9	9	District Office (meetings, task forces, reports, etc.)	6	6
7	6	Professional Development (reading, conferences, etc.)	9	9
4	5	Planning (annual, long-range)	7	7

The principals who spent time as they intended credited these reasons: ability to delegate; capable assistant principals; faith in competence of others; and concentration upon priority goals. Even the effective principals, however, considered these strategies as incomplete in the face of growing demands on time from all sides together with the ever-present need to be visible to students, staff, and parents.

The allocation of time is difficult for any busy executive, including the principal. Typically, a principal finds the needs and expectations of others pushing upon his own priorities. These expectations range from the personal problems of students and teachers faced daily to the weekly cycle of events and activities and special programs, to the monthly cycle of scheduled meetings and reports, to the yearly calendar with its evolving expectations from September to December to June. These four levels of demand, operating simultaneously and often interrupted by unscheduled crises and demands, can send the principal spinning unless he is solidly alert to his own schedule of priorities. This schedule must include the delegation to others of sufficient responsibilities to ensure the accomplishment of important tasks retained by the principal.

Effective principals consider district meetings, paperwork, and referral of unresolved problems as their "biggest time wasters." Some important initiatives, then, must be taken at the local, state, and national levels to cut the number of formal meetings, the volume of routine paperwork, and the quantity of reports. In addition, only the more serious problems and appeals should be heard by the principal. For the principal this requires the self-discipline to insist that assistant administrators make decisions within policy, and then to support those decisions. It also requires recognition by boards of education and by superintendents that significant new demands have been thrust upon principals over the past seven or eight years by legislation, court decisions, board rulings, and collective bargaining agreements. To meet these demands, each school must be assigned an adequate administrative and secretarial staff, or the more important priorities such as program improvement will atrophy.

ROLE EXPECTATIONS

Compounding the problem of job responsibilities is the finding that the referent groups (parents, students, teachers, board members) apparently understand very little about the ways a principal actually spends time week by week. Students were the most knowledgeable, but generally all "significant other" groups believe a principal spends more time on (1) planning, (2) school management, and (3) professional development than he actually does spend, and that he spends less time on personnel and community affairs than the job requires. Teachers, in fact, consider the district office as ranking third in time demands upon the principal, whereas district office personnel rank their demands as eighth in line. The principal cuts between these figures, placing it fifth in order of time spent. With differences of this magnitude, a picture emerges of the principal operating in obscurity, void of accurate perceptions by the very people with whom he works week by week. Obviously this situation benefits no one, so joint clarifications of perception must be placed high on the priority list.

Understanding the situational factors of the job constitutes a first important step to this clarification because the "significant others" and the effective principals agree on the way a principal's time *should* be allocated to job responsibilities. It is not clear at this point whether differences in perception about the way a principal actually spends time are the result of a variety of role expectations, or whether they result simply from the various viewpoints represented. The differences, however, are significant.

CONSTRAINTS AND RESOURCES

The effective principals operate generally under the same job constraints as the random sample group. The constraints most frequently mentioned include inadequate resources, master contracts, incompetent teachers, federal and state regulations, interruptions in work schedules, and lack of adequate administrative assistance.[1]

Both groups of principals also report that their respective district offices provide similar degrees of latitude in such matters as budget allocation and teacher employment. Their authority and participation in these matters are reported in Table 2[2].

TABLE 2
Budget Allocations

Participation on determining budget allocation	Percent	
	Effectives	Random
High participation	34	37
Moderate participation	29	30
Little participation	22	21
No participation	14	12

Hiring of Teachers

Authority to fill teacher vacancy	Percent	
	Effectives	Random
I make the selection and the central office endorses it.	55	51
I make a selection within limited options given by the central office.	42	41
The central office selects the teacher to fill the vacancy.	3	8

Here, however, similarities between the effective and the random sample principals apparently end. *Perceptions* of the effective group are that they face fewer administrative roadblocks and fewer constraints generally than does the random sample group. For example, the effective principals see the central office as more supportive and not as constraining when compared to opinions of the random sample group. Table 3 summarizes this outlook.

19

---

[1]In addition to the on-site interviews, a separate study of effective principals and their relationship to the random sample group was conducted by Nancy De Leonibus, using the survey questionnaire developed for Volume I. Her findings, in addition to those reported here, are contained in the unpublished doctoral dissertation entitled "A Comparative Study of Two Groups of High School Principals on Selected Personal, Professional, School, Staff, and Student Characteristics," American University, Washington, D.C., 1978.

[2]The data illustrating differences between the effective group and the random sample group in this report come from the comparative study by Nancy De Leonibus, research associate at NASSP.

TABLE 3
Roadblocks to Administration (Central Office)

Central Office/ School Board	Not a Constraint		Minor Constraint		Major Constraint	
	Effectives	Random	Effectives	Random	Effectives	Random
Policy restrictions	38	37	52	51	10	11
Lack of support	59	55	38	31	3	13
Interference	62	49	36	37	2	13

Within the school setting, itself, some interesting differences in outlook arise between the two sets of principals pertaining to teachers and students.

TABLE 4
Roadblocks to Administration (School Site)

Teacher Factors	Not a Factor		Somewhat a Factor		Serious Factor	
	Effectives	Random	Effectives	Random	Effectives	Random
Variations in ability and dedication of teachers . . .	24	15	71	65	5	18
Tendency of older teachers to frown on new methods . . .	66	44	28	46	7	10

Student Factors	Not a Constraint		Minor Constraint		Major Constraint	
	Effectives	Random	Effectives	Random	Effectives	Random
Absenteeism	28	25	53	47	19	27
Lack of motivation	7	10	76	56	16	33
Discipline Problems	32	26	61	62	7	11

The lack of sufficient administrative staff at the school appears to be a serious problem for the typical principal as contrasted to the exemplary group. Some 41 percent of the effective principals describe the number of administrative staff as "fully adequate" while only 28 percent of the random sample group agreed. Both groups of principals, however, describe the *quality* of assistance as good.

The matter of constraints, then, appears to be a mixed bag. All principals face certain restrictions involving resources, personnel, and board policy. These constraints are common to the job. The severity of constraint, however, appears greater to the typical principal on these factors than it does to the sample group of effective principals. Especially in the area of interpersonal relationships with immediate associates—teachers, students, and central office—does the effective principal see fewer constraints than does the random sample group.

The effective principals generally believe their schools are better staffed administratively than does the random sample group. This suggests that one factor contributing to high effectiveness could be an adequate staffing of assistant principals.

When asked what job conditions contributed to job effectiveness, the effective principals listed most frequently: (1) a quality, supportive staff, (2) cooperative, energetic students, (3) encouragement by the central office, (4) community support, and (5) job autonomy. Each referent group considers itself as important to the principal's job success. The groups, however, rated their own support at a higher value than they were rated by others. Teachers, central office, and the parents each placed themselves first in the list of "job conditions especially helpful to the principal." Students rated themselves third.

The "significant others" were not pollyanna about the matter, however, as each tended to identify its own group as causing constraints. Students, for instance, cited themselves and the community as constraints for the principal, while parents cited community apathy and the board of education. Teachers, in contrast, said the central office was a major constraint.

In summary, supportive and cooperative people with whom the principal works, together with sufficient job autonomy and an adequate administrative staff, appear to be important keys to effectiveness. Perceived job constraints tend also to focus upon people relationships at all levels. It is for good reason, indeed, that the effective principal places a high priority upon the ability to work effectively with people. The school administrator works literally through people, and he must develop competence in this area to be effective.

Job Attack

As a leader, the effective principal approaches problems directly, sets high standards, establishes an open and accepting climate, and works to develop new practices in the school. He moves actively toward the solution of problems, involving those people affected by the problem along the way. He initiates improvements in program and school management, but also provides resources to the initiatives of others, especially teachers. He is, in sum, both composer and conductor of resources in the school.

PROBLEM SOLVING

Effective principals rate themselves high on problem-solving ability. This good rating gains the concurrence of the "significant others" groups, all of whom assign the principal a 4.5 on a five-point scale. They agree their principal can and does solve problems competently.

The technique employed to solve problems involves: (1) gathering and discussing facts openly with all parties concerned, and (2) making decisions mutually acceptable to the parties concerned. Decisions normally are made as soon as the facts are known. Timing is important. When principals were asked to describe instances of poor problem solving, typical responses included: "I waited too long"; "I acted impulsively"; "I didn't weigh all the possibilities."

Parents and students placed a high value on "fair and prompt" problem solving. Few "significant others" could cite problems they considered to be poorly handled by their principal, however. These referent groups lacked knowledge about specific problem-solving actions by the principal. The few examples given involved persons from their own reference group only. The "significant others" groups also had difficulty describing the processes used by a principal to solve problems. Rather, they credited personal qualities of the principal (fairness, judgment, patience) for his effectiveness as a problem solver.

The principals, however, tended to credit their success to a process of thorough investigation and extensive involvement with problems; although they noted that problem solving is also situational and requires judgment and timing based upon the factors at hand.

Each "significant other" group wanted problems solved within its own frame of reference (i.e., teachers wanted support and firm discipline, central office wanted policy to be followed, etc.). The principals placed the highest value on none of these, but rather on resolving problems related to the educational program of the school. Secondly, they attended to problems of student behavior; and, thirdly, to problems of school management. It is interesting that the referent groups are unaware of the initiatives and problem resolutions acted upon by the effective principals most frequently, yet they believe these principals to be highly competent at problem resolution. Perhaps in those discrete areas where the principal is observed by the various referent groups, he solves problems sufficiently well for the reputation to become generalized.

Whatever the task area, most problems faced by the principal involve interpersonal conflict. The effective principal as problem solver, therefore, must be skilled in human relations. Applying these skills, the road to resolution is: "Get the full story, listen well, and then have the courage and the luck to make the right decisions," or "Act as soon as you are fully informed." Intuitive factors apparently play a large part in problem solving, once the fact-gathering step is completed. The laborious "scientific approach" to problem solving is short circuited by intuitive judgment.

In summary, the effective principal doesn't perceive problems as terribly severe; he believes problems can be solved, recognizes that he can't solve problems by himself, involves the persons affected in resolution of the problem, and initiates change in anticipation of finessing problems which may emerge. No single "style" is used, but initiative and involvement are common elements with effective principals.

PROGRAM DEVELOPMENT

Most effective principals are engaged in developing curriculum and improving instruction, rating their competency as a 4.0 on the five-point scale. Parents give them a high mark of 5.0 while the central office rates their curriculum effectiveness at 4.5. Teachers agree with principals that 4.0 is accurate. Obviously effective principals carry a good image as knowledgeable and competent educators.

Effective principals place high value on a flexible, growing educational environment. Asked about the strengths of their curriculum, the effective principals most commonly answered, "comprehensive choices for every student," "flexibility," "balance of college prep and non-college prep," "strong academics and honors," and "many choices."

This interest is reflected in Table 5 which shows high percentages of students in the schools lead by effective principals participating in various alternatives for credit to graduation in addition to summer school.

TABLE 5
Student Options for Credit

Options	Percent of Schools Offering Option	
	Effectives	Random
Night, adult school, or correspondence courses	78	61
College level courses taught at your school	40	24
College courses taught at a college	64	46
Credit by examination	34	18
Credit by contract and independent study	76	55
Off-campus work experience/on-the-job training	83	61
Community volunteer programs	34	17

Effective principals depend upon a heavy involvement of subject area departments and of individual faculty members for curriculum development. Here ideas originate, goals are identified, plans are laid, materials are developed, and resources committed. The central office provides the overall curricular plan and consultants. Moderate participation comes from curriculum committees—usually in the form of needs assessment—and from community and student participants. No single role was played by the principals other than as initiator and/or as implementor.

The effective principal considers himself an important change agent. Needs are identified, ideas are planted, resources are provided, suggestions are made, persons are involved. Again, the "significant others" carry a different perspective by seeing the principal in a static and not a dynamic role as regards change. They don't view him as a planner, consultant, or evaluator of change in the school. This outlook may result from the principal often working through (or with) others to accomplish objectives.

Imposed changes by federal and state legislatures or board action are only about half as frequent as changes initiated by the professional staff together with the principal.

Most of the effective principals anticipate needs by planning on an annual or a three-year basis. Such planning includes: (1) survey of student needs, (2) discussion with faculty, (3) review of student requests, (4) reviewing professional literature and attending professional meetings, and (5) preparing for mandated requirements.

The principals acknowledge evaluation of program to be a weakness and rate themselves as a "3" on the five-point scale. Generally they depend upon the central office or university consultants for a formal evaluation, or upon teachers and students for informal feedback. Of all administrative tasks, principals rated themselves lowest in program evaluation.

DECISION MAKING

Effective principals believe that school climate and institutional esprit are directly affected by their own actions. They exercise considerable influence over the atmosphere of their school by establishing the quality of human relationships and by building confidence and trust.

As chief decision maker, the effective principal anticipates and influences the direction of planning. But he involves the staff and students in these plans. Once initiated, the principal usually steps back to guide and monitor a project rather than to continue as a dominant leader.

Faculty influence in decision making is high, ranking 4.0 on a five-point scale. All "significant others" concur in this ranking. The effective principals also rate high in staff relations, again ranking 4.0 in the opinion of all groups.

Inservice education is tied to school improvement projects, again giving evidence of effective planning and coordination.

While the referent groups agree that effective principals are capable decision makers and that they enjoy good staff relations, little is known about the principal's operating style. They cannot describe, for instance, the principal's approach to planning and initiating projects in the school. They know he is involved, but they do not know the specifics of this involvement. They know he is effective, but they cannot describe the reasons for this effectiveness beyond listing personality traits.

One aspect of student opinion is especially intriguing. Parents and students agree that the students' greatest interests concern the future, especially jobs and/or college. The principals and teachers, however, believe that school-related matters such as grades, activities, and social relationships constitute the greatest concerns of students. Possibly students are not involved sufficiently in program development to convey their interests clearly to the professional staff or else the students' immediate participation in school events masks an underlying concern about their future status.

Effective principals consider four initiatives as critical to good school morale. These include:

- Recognize teaching as important by providing attention and acknowledgement to the faculty.

- Respond to teacher and student concerns. Show interest. Be available.

- Provide for participation and involvement. Include staff and students in the major issues.

- Provide an equitable work load for teachers. Cut time demands whenever possible.

STUDENT RELATIONSHIPS

While the majority of effective principals do not maintain formal contact with student organizations week by week, they do place a high value on cultivating good communication with student leaders. Typically the discussion involves student activities and school rules rather than curriculum.

For influencing students positively effective principals set high expectations, provide for participation, develop new activities and programs, and meet emerging problems straight on. They are as visible to students as possible, given the time restraints of the job. They communicate informally whenever possible with students.

These 60 effective principals would like to be perceived by students as "a friend and leader," "someone who works for a better school," "a firm but fair person," and "a person who helps them to develop pride in themselves and their school."

PARENTAL AND COMMUNITY RELATIONSHIPS

About two-thirds of the effective principals involve parents in goal setting, policy advising, or curriculum planning. This is a significantly higher involvement than with the random sample group of principals.

The same pattern carries over to the operation of schools. The effective principals tend to use parents more as volunteers and resource persons than do principals generally, but not more as sponsors of student groups or as monitors of student activities.

TABLE 6
Parental Involvement

	Percent	
Type of Activity	Effectives	Random
Objectives and Priorities	74	58
Program Changes/New Programs	72	55
Student Behavior Policies	59	50
Evaluation of Programs	47	36

The effective principals appear to enjoy good relationships generally with parents. Only about 10 percent of the effective principals consider "apathetic and irresponsible parents" as serious roadblocks for the administration, whereas twice that number of the random sample group consider apathetic parents as roadblocks. The majority of both groups of principals, however, consider irresponsible or apathetic parents as "somewhat" of a roadblock to administering a school.

Parents saw their contribution to curriculum development as more important than contributions made by students or the central office. These two groups, in turn, saw their contributions as the most helpful to principals.

No distinctive approach to communicating with parents could be identified. The effective principals use a mix of written and spoken communication of all kinds. They prepare the way through informal communications and then follow-up with structured information, again monitoring the effectiveness of formal procedures with informal discussion.

LEADERSHIP AND OPERATIONAL SKILLS

Effective principals display a variety of leadership styles. They tend to involve others to accomplish tasks, they set standards and provide an example by their hard work, and they make decisions at appropriate times. But beyond these few similarities the effective principals apply an idiosyncratic style to lead their schools. They make a difference in their schools by utilizing their own style. Effective principals agree that they enjoy wide opportunity for leadership and that this is a central satisfaction of the job.

Their ability to relate well to other people ("People like me," "I make people feel at ease"), a trait noted by the effective principals and confirmed by all the referent groups, provides the base from which the effective principals work. But beyond using this base, no single approach is used. They are consistent in their inconsistency. The effective principals get into fine detail in one situation but stay at a strategic level in another. They delegate enthusiastically at one time and sparsely

26

the next time. They may be close and supportive on one task and more demanding about another. They communicate sometimes orally and sometimes in writing. They may spend weeks analyzing one problem yet move abruptly on another. They may listen in one meeting and talk incessantly during another.

What the effective principal does is *perceive differences* from situation to situation. He analyzes the actions required and then moves toward a decision based on that analysis. While the effective principal does involve the people affected and does rely upon good interpersonal relationships, his leadership style is contingent more upon an analysis of the situation at hand than on routine procedures. He is perceptive about the persons and conditions relating to his job. The effective principal relies upon the "leadership style" he considers appropriate and efficient to the situation.

On a more personal level, an entire arsenal of talents is applied to leadership demands placed on the principalship. Among the more frequent suggestions are these: "Set an example," "Be committed to quality," "Work at good human relationships," "Know the community," "Have a good mental attitude and physical stamina," "Be committed to the staff and school," "Compromise to get agreement," "Maintain poise," "Be able to handle stress," "Create a structure for things to happen," "Admit mistakes," "Don't take conflict personally," "Lead from a positive approach," "Don't get too far ahead of the people you lead," "Be available to people," and "Have an understanding family."

Effective principals do not consider stress a major problem. Their suggestions for handling stress include keeping a good sense of perspective, "getting away," and involving oneself in recreation.

Personal and Professional Characteristics

The effective principals ranged in age from 30 to over 60 years but almost half were in their 40s. In college they usually majored in the social sciences or secondarily in the sciences and humanities. Fourteen percent graduated in physical education. Eighty percent received honors or prizes in college.

They participated broadly in college athletics and activities. This tendency toward involvement continues into their adult life as they collectively carry 137 memberships in 47 different organizations ranging from churches to service clubs to the American Dutch Rabbit Club.

The effective principals are active in professional organizations, both state and national, participating at about twice the rate of the random sample group. They frequently make presentations but author only an occasional article. One-sixth have taught courses or conducted workshops at colleges or universities.

Effective principals also tend to refer professional literature frequently to faculty members, committees, and department chairmen. Their use of the literature in this way is also about double that of the random sample group.

Over 30 percent of the effective principals have earned the doctorate as compared to nine percent of the random sample group. Conversely, 12 percent of the random sample have no education beyond the master's degree compared with zero percent of the effective group.

Some difference of opinion exists between the effective and random sample groups about the value of professional courses. For instance, the psychology of learning is considered "essential" by 59 percent of the effective group as compared to 38 percent of the random sample; leadership is felt to be "essential" by 76 percent of the effective group as compared to 63 percent of the random sample; and human relations is rated "essential" by 84 percent of the effective group as compared to 71 percent of the random sample. Some courses, however, are rated as more essential by the random sample group. These include school finance and budgeting, negotiations, and personnel administration. Other courses ranked high by both groups include school law, internship experience, curriculum development, school management, and community relations. Eighteen percent of the random sample considered history of education "of no use" compared with three percent of the effective principals.

The most common career route was through the assistant principalship at a high school or junior high school. Effective principals tended to be appointed to their first principalship at a relatively young age, with 36 percent becoming principals by age 30. Only 22 percent of the random sample group were principals by this age. The effective principals also appear to be quite mobile, with over 30 percent holding three or more principalships, double that of the random sample group.

Job security appears of little concern to the effective principals. Almost half rank their security as very high (at point "5" on a scale of one to five). Only five percent rank their security as a low "1" or "2" on the scale as compared with 17 percent of the random sample. Effective principals believe also that latitude for independent thought and action is good and that they enjoy considerable prestige. Eighty-five percent of the effective principals rate their prestige as a "4" or "5" on the five-point scale, as contrasted to 65 percent of the random sample group.

When asked: "Does the principalship offer the opportunity to fulfill one's unique capabilities?" the principals answered with a resounding "yes," with 82 percent giving a "4" or "5" rating to this question. Yet many are considering other positions, with 19 percent of the effective principals interested in a university position and 40 percent interested in a central office job or a superintendency. Only five percent of the random sample group were inclined toward college work while 33 percent are inclined toward the central office. About one third of both groups are committed to the principalship as a career position.

Enhancing Effectiveness

It would be presumptuous to assert that the keys to effectiveness are all contained in these studies. Yet, effective principals exhibit some common behaviors and express some common opinions that provide insight about proficiency in the position. While acknowledging that leadership is situational and that school situations vary widely from community to community, this study suggests the principalship may be strengthened by these means:

1. *Personal and Professional Factors*
    Attention must be given to encouraging and selecting the best talent available to enter the principalship. Professional education beyond the master's degree apparently is beneficial as is experience in an assistant principalship or similar position. An ability to work with people—all different kinds of people—is central to effectiveness as is adaptability to various situations. An ability to motivate professional staff, students, and parents to accomplish tasks is important. So is dedication to the interests of students and long hours of work.
    Outlook may also be important since effective principals perceive few insurmountable constraints. An ability to perceive and resolve problems evidently is critical as is an adequate sense of timing for decisions. A professional growth activity such as participating in professional meetings or reading and using professional literature apparently enhances effectiveness. Job mobility is no deterrent.

2. *Situational Factors*
    The effective principals, when asked what factors assisted their effectiveness, indicated these conditions as important: (1) a high quality teaching staff, (2) a cooperative and interested community, (3) a receptive school climate, (4) an excellent student body, (5) a strong administrative staff and a supportive central office. Evidently the contributions of all referent groups are considered necessary to an optimum situation.
    The "significant others" groups had few suggestions for making the principalship more operative; the question apparently is not an issue with the parents, students, teachers, and central office personnel associated with the effective principals. Their few recommendations involved greater principal contact; i.e., students said to spend more time with students.
    The principalship must be better understood by its consti-

tuency. The referent groups have to be more perceptive about the principal's broad scope of responsibilities and operating procedures, and the principal must do a better job of communicating these factors. The principalship is made more difficult by remaining mysterious than by becoming understood.

When asked what changes would make the principalship more effective than at present, the principals expressed this collective opinion: (1) Provide more autonomy—allow the individual school to exercise more authority for decision making; (2) Clarify the role—review job descriptions and clarify expectations with the different referent groups to gain *common* expectations; (3) Reduce the volume of paperwork and meetings—require only the most necessary reports and meetings; (4) Include the principal's viewpoint in policy—when a faculty and student body are affected by policy, the principal's advice is important to good policy formulation; (5) Provide inservice education on modern management, staff evaluation, program evaluation, and on current trends and issues.

3. *Administrative Processes*

As could be expected, the effective principals rate high on task initiative as well as on the maintenance of good interpersonal relationships. For example, the effective principal utilizes a strong human relations capability to achieve the task objectives of the institution. He seldom if ever goes ahead alone; he prefers to move ahead together.

The effective principal initiates as well as responds; supports as well as questions; and approves as well as challenges. He has a piece of the significant changes taking place in the school.

He can identify and solve problems. While no single approach is used to problem resolution, normally that resolution includes the involvement of the people affected. His commitment to involvement as a means of solving problems is not appreciated by constituents who, rather, see personal qualities of fairness and honesty as reasons for his success.

The effective principal leadership style is contingent upon perceptions of the situation. He follows no model slavishly but rather acts intuitively within the general guidelines of broad involvement, full fact gathering, appropriate timing, and time efficiency.

In these many factors the effective principal tends not to be so different in kind from principals selected randomly. Rather, the difference is one of degree—he works harder, perceives better, involves extensively, participates widely, initiates often, manages efficiently, delegates frequently, communicates effectively and enjoys strong community support. He is optimistic in outlook and he minimizes constraints even while acknowledging they exist. He is committed to the school and its tasks and enjoys the challenge of accomplishing those tasks.

3 The Private and Religious School Principal

PRIVATE, RELIGIOUS, AND RELIGIOUS-AFFILIATED schools make up more than 13 percent of the nation's high schools; and the principals of these schools represent a major leadership influence in American education. Because of smaller average enrollments, the numbers of students served may be closer to 10 percent, although only estimates are available from the NASSP study and other sources. Beyond its significance in terms of size, the private education sector is a valued segment of American secondary education; and the status, welfare, and problems of these principals are an important concern.

The National Study of the High School Principalship included private and religious principals in its survey and its in-depth study of effective principals. The survey data relative to private, religious, and religious-affiliated school principals were analyzed separately and as a group in order to make comparisons between public and private/religious schools and among various sub samples. This chapter deals with relevant findings from the survey, the effective principals study, and from separate investigations conducted by the research staff. It treats the characteristics of the school, the job, the principal, and the principals' perceptions of educational tasks, issues and practices, and the future.

Principals of private and religious schools often express opinions about the differences among their schools and between them and public schools. Data from the NASSP study permit examination of similarities and differences in an objective fashion for the first time, and these data provide a baseline for longitudinal studies of the factors treated. Therefore, where appropriate, comparisons are made; however, a reportorial-commentary style is employed to avoid the presentation of large amounts of factual information.

33

The Private and Religious or Religious-affiliated High School

The term "private school sector" is used to designate all nonpublic schools whether private, parochial, religious, or religious affiliated. Also, the term religious is used to designate all religious and religious-affiliated schools of whatever type or denomination. However, only schools and principals were included in the study in which the school had a twelfth-grade graduating class—this being the criterion used to designate a high school. Interestingly, in both public and private sectors the three-year high school terminating with grade 11 disappeared from the educational scene during the past 15 years. Also, unlike the public sector, private and religious high schools are almost universally four-year institutions, some being K-12 or 1-12 grades.

The *percentage* of private sector schools has declined since the early 1960s. (Data for NASSP's 1965 study were collected in 1962-63.) Private sector schools declined in ratio to public schools from approximately 17 percent to 13.9 percent in 1977. Whether the actual number of schools has declined is uncertain because an increase in the number of public schools during this period alone might account for the change, and absolute numbers of all types of schools are not available.

The largest percentage of private sector high schools exists in states on the west coast, 22.2 percent of all high schools of that region; New England states, 21.5 percent; and mid Atlantic states, 21.3 percent. The percentage declines to only 2.8 percent in the intermountain region. The midwest has the largest number of private sector schools. This is so because, even though this region has only 12.1 percent of its total as private or religious schools, the region contains 37.4 percent of all the high schools of the nation.

In terms of school size, two-thirds of all private schools have enrollments under 500 students; while of the religious schools 40 percent of the parochial and almost 60 percent of the remainder of the religious-affiliated group have enrollments under 500. The dramatic increase in size of school experienced in the public sector did not occur in the private sector. In 1965, 63 percent of *all* high schools of the nation had enrollments under 500 students; by 1977, this percentage had declined to 23.8 percent. However, the number of small private and religious schools remained almost constant, and their proportion of small schools was 60.9 percent of all the small schools of the nation.

The size factor appears to be an artifact of several conditions and is responsible for differences between principals in the public and the private sectors. Cost and availability of clientele are definite factors, but in the case of many private schools and schools that are religious affiliated but non-parochial, a conscious choice was made not to alter the character and mission of the school by increasing its size. Particularly in the East and parts of the South, where private schools and certain religious schools are selective and college-prep oriented, decisions were made to resist increasing size.

Size produces some important effects for principals. Principals in smaller schools are much more likely to hold regular teaching assignments. (More than 80 percent of the private and more than 40 percent of the religious versus only 10 percent of the public school principals teach.) Principals indicate significantly more concern for teaching competence, value program and instructional leadership more highly, and maintain a wider scope of authority over decision functions than their public school counterparts—even when compared to a sample of principals of small public high schools. Some of these factors are treated later in this chapter.

The Principalship in the Private and Religious School

The treatment of grouped data relative to private sector schools in terms of the job of the principal reveals some real differences with the public school principalship. The private sector principalship as already pointed out usually entails a regular teaching assignment and much more authority in certain decision functions: hiring and dismissal of personnel, budget planning and reallocation of funds, use of discretionary funds, and in program determination. These principals report being less affected by outside interest groups (with the exception of religious outside groups being much more influential in religious school matters), fewer "road blocks" to performance of duties (administrative detail, funds, competence of teachers, etc.), much higher personal rewards, and more administrative assistance in proportion to the size of school.

There is high agreement within the group of religious and religious-affiliated principals on all the points noted above. Among the private school principals, however, there is a bi-modal distribution of measures relative to several of these factors and others which are noted later. Apparently within the private school group there are well established schools, strongly supported by parents, and those which are marginal in funding and size which may be struggling for survival. The former group is in strong agreement with the points noted above, while the latter indicates much greater problems of funding, inadequate administrative assistance, and less discretionary authority. The future concerns of this group of principals with general economic conditions, declining enrollments, and pressures of outside interest groups seem to indicate that a worsening of these conditions might well create crises in these schools.

Heavy time demands of the job are clearly evident. The private sector principals' average work week is 54 hours, with the religious principals' work week at 54-plus hours, and the private school principals' work week at 52.5 hours. Independent checks and other sources confirm these figures to be conservative. Excessively long hours are spent dealing with administrative details, planning, and meeting professionally after the normal school day and an average of two evenings weekly at school-related activities or meetings. Surprisingly, all groups of "significant others" (parents, central office, students, and teachers)

35

know that the principal does spend long hours, but they do not evidence a concern that such demands are a threat to the quality of school life or to the principal as a professional person.

Picking up the point about others' perceptions of the principal, evidence from the effective principal study indicates a serious dilemma. Groups understood very little about the actual job conditions of the principal—the nature of the work, pressures and problems, conditions that might facilitate the overall climate of the school, etc. On the other hand, principals universally expressed concerns about these job conditions to the investigators, and a serious loss of effective principals to the profession was documented because of them; that is, approximately 15 percent indicated that they had already arranged to leave the principalship for the next year, and an additional 15 percent said that they would definitely leave by the following year.

Allocation of time to categories of activities provided rankings which are shown in Table 1. Religious-affiliated (RAS) and private (Pri) school principals were separated to show differences which occurred between these groups and their public school (PS) counterparts. Rankings are shown for both actual and ideal ratings.

TABLE 1
Allocation of Time by Principals for A Typical Work Week

Area of Responsibility	Should Spend Time			Do Spend Time		
	RAS	Pri	PS	RAS	Pri	PS
Program Development	1	1	1	4	6	5
Personnel	2	3	2	2	2	2
School Management	3	2	3	1	1	1
Student Activities	4	5	4	3	3	3
Planning (long range)	5	4	5	7	8	7
Professional Development	6	7	6	9	7	9
Student Behavior	7	6	7	5	4	4
Community	8	8	8	6	5	8
District Office	9	9	9	8	9	6

36

Principals actually spend most of their time on things they think they should but in a somewhat different order in terms of amount of time actually spent. The religious-affiliated (RAS) principals and the public school (PS) principals indicate little difference in how they allocate time and how they believe they should. The private school principals show the largest number of differences both from the other two groups and between how they actually spend time and how they would like to spend it. Private school principals indicate that they spend less time on program development and more time on community functions and on professional development than do the other two groups of principals. All groups placed management as their number-one time consumer, but all groups would like to allocate the most time to program development.

No significant differences appear on rankings between men and women principals in any of the three groups, although women principals ranked planning higher than the men did. Some other differences occurred in percentages which did not shift the rankings. For example, management—ranked first by all three groups—was ranked first by 54 percent of the public school principals, 68 percent of the private school principals, and 74 percent of the religious principals. The teaching function also was not included in the rating, but data already presented indicate the significant amount of time devoted to teaching by private and religious school principals versus their public school counterparts.

Although satisfaction with the job is high, the position for all private sector principals holds heavy time demands and is impacted by pressures and problems, this does not permit the principal to control the allocation of effort as these principals would like. Along with these conditions, the evidence indicates that "significant others" do not understand the conditions inherent in the job. Since work conditions cannot be improved without the understanding and support of superiors, patrons, teachers, and students, it is likely that these conditions will persist and schools will continue to experience an inordinate loss of the more effective principals.

Characteristics of the Principal

The private, religious, and public school principals differ in terms of age, tenure, age of first principalship, and amount of teaching experience. The private school principal is younger (38), was appointed to his first principalship at a younger age (34), has less tenure in his current position (five years), has more teaching experience (16 years), and has held fewer principalships (more than 80 percent have held only one principalship—their current one). The bi-modal distribution referred to earlier in terms of the private school principal appears here in that the private school principal is either quite young (under 35) or in his mid-50s with few cases beyond those who cluster in these age groups.

The average religious school principal is 43-years-old, has taught 12.5 years, was appointed at age 37, has held two principalships, and has six years in the principalship—four years in the current position. One striking difference between the religious principals and other groups is that 43 percent of these principals are women versus seven percent in the public sector and only one percent in the private schools—the latter figure may be biased because of the small number of private schools in the sample. The woman religious principal is older—46 years compared to 41 years for the men. She was appointed at a later age (38), has more teaching experience (16 years—10 years for the men), and has held only one principalship.

To provide a comparison, the public school principal is 46 years of age, has taught 9.5 years, received his first principalship at age 35, has served 10 years as a principal with six years in his current position. Unlike his counterpart in the private sector, the route to the public school principalship is almost always through an assistant principalship in the district where he received his first principalship.

The preparation of principals in the private sector is quite diversified at both undergraduate and graduate levels. Eighty-one percent of the religious principals majored in humanities, basic sciences, and social sciences at the undergraduate level, while the private school principals majored in humanities, social sciences, math, and business, in that order. Educational administration dominates at the graduate level (39%) but not as completely as for the public school principal (76%). The humanities is a preferred area of study for principals in the private sector at the undergraduate level and is in second place at the graduate level. Apparently a generally accepted point of view in the private sector is that a broad general background is more important than a particular specialty.

Even though diversity is characteristic of the educational background of private sector principals, they have acquired training in administration during graduate study and are aware of what is necessary for successful performance. Principals were asked to rate 24 courses in terms of utility for the beginning principal. With a criterion that 90 percent of the sample must rate a course as highly useful or essential, the list which is shown in Table 2 resulted.

38

TABLE 2
Principals' Evaluation of Importance of Course Work, Rankings

Course	Private Sector	Public
Curriculum and Program Planning	1	3
School Management	2	2
Human Relations	3	5
Supervision of Instruction	4	4
Finance and Budgeting	5	6
Leadership	6	9
Principalship	7	7

Public school principals ranked school law and personnel administration within the 90 percent criterion, probably showing the concern of public school principals for the need to deal with the many changed legal requirements and the need to deal with teacher unions. However, the high agreement (90 percent level) and the unanimity between public and private sector principals provides some evidence of common problems and needs. A separate examination of female respondents from the private sector reveals that women principals indicated a statistically greater percentage of rankings of courses as highly useful or essential; they seemed to consider all course work to be relatively more important than did the men.

Finally, more than 75 percent of all private sector principals have graduate course work beyond the master's, although less than two percent hold doctorates versus 12 percent for public sector principals. More than 70 percent of these principals rate job satisfaction high, and they would again choose educational administration as a career.

Educational Practices, Issues, and Program Priorities

The views of principals relative to certain educational practices and issues impacting high schools and the perceived priorities for the high school educational program were examined. Groups of principals were gathered to identify such practices and issues in the preparation of the survey instruments in addition to the usual literature searches and consultations undertaken by the research team. Responses from principals of private sector schools were strikingly similar in many instances.

Rank order is provided in the table in the order, from 1 to 11, of the responses of RAS principals. Agreement within the three groups of principals was high. Even the women and men principals within the groups were quite similar. Within the RAS principal group only three items were statistically different. The women rank "development of self concept . . ." closer to 1, while the men rank "acquisition of basic skills" and "development of skills to operate a technological society" closer to 1 than did women principals. Pri principals appear to partially agree with the RAS principals and partially with the PS principals. Except for items (a), (d), and (h) the rank order between Pri and RAS principals is the same in terms of rank order. Except for items (c), (e), (h), and (i) the Pri and PS principals are basically the same in terms of rank order. It is apparent that RAS principals believe the most important tasks involve moral, intellectual, and aesthetic areas with less emphasis upon practical-vocational and personal areas. The Pri principal tends to favor intellectual, moral, and aesthetic areas as well, but the latter two much less strongly. Personal and practical-vocational are

TABLE 3
Ranking of Educational Tasks

Tasks	RAS Rank	Pri Rank	PS Rank
a. Development of moral and spiritual values	1	3	4
b. Acquisition of basic skills	2	1	1
c. Development of positive self-concept and good human relations	3	4	2
d. Development of skills and practices of critical intellectual inquiry and problem solving	4	2	3
e. Appreciation for and experience with the fine arts	5	6	11
f. Preparation for a changing world	6	7	8
g. Knowledge about and skills in preparation for family life	7	8	6
h. Career planning and training in specific "entry level" occupational skills	8	12	5
i. Understanding of the American value system (political, economic, social values)	9	9	7
j. Physical fitness and useful leisure time sports	10	10	9
k. Development of the skills to operate a technological society (engineering, scientific)	11	11	10

also ranked lowest, but practical-vocational much less preferred by the Pri than the RAS principal.

No differences of opinion among the religious and the private school principals relative to broad educational issues exist except in two cases. Religious principals agree, with many reservations, that "limitations should be placed upon classroom discussion of political "isms" and "anti-isms" and that the compulsory academic year should be lengthened—on these items they are in agreement with public school principals. However, private school principals disagree regarding both statements. All groups agree, without reservation, that special programs should be developed for educating academically talented, handicapped, and ethnic minority students. They also agree, with some reservations, that student rights in matters of due process, confidentiality of student and staff records, and equal treatment of the sexes (Title IX) are positive and necessary developments in secondary schools.

The greatest difference of opinion is noted in reference to "Federal aid must be made available to private and religious secondary schools." For this issue the majority of private sector principals agree without reservation, while the majority of public school principals disagree. Although significantly different (beyond the .01 level, using the standard error of proportions as the statistic) other issues do not mirror such extreme positions.

Private sector principals indicate more unqualified agreement with

"Court decisions concerning racial segregation are correct as they apply to public schools" and "Schools should provide a general intellectual background and leave specific job training to other agencies."

Conversely, the public school principals indicate more unqualified agreement with "Schools require far too little academic work of students" and "Youths who are disinterested or hostile toward schooling should *not* be required to attend."

Private sector principals tend to show unqualified disagreement with these issue statements: "There is a need to justify as practical each subject taught;" "Court decisions concerning compulsory prayer and Bible reading are correct;" and "School attendance should be compulsory until high school graduation or age 18." Public school principals tend toward agreement with these issue statements although their responses indicate a split or middle position.

Perceptions of the Future

Principals indicated opinions about the influence of certain conditions or developments over the next three to five years. All groups of principals agree that "desegregation" and "a national youth service" will have no influence on high schools. Apparently they feel that the adjustments and arrangements to deal with desegregation are pretty much worked out. They also all agree that "enrollment declines," "community based learning," "community participation," and "new technology" will have a moderate influence. There is universal agreement that "staff competency" will have a strong influence.

Finance and the general economy is seen as a strong influence by all groups, but much stronger for religious principals than public school principals and even stronger for private school principals. Neither religious-affiliated nor private school principals see as an influence: "student non-attendance," "alternative schools," or "lowering of compulsory attendance age"; however public school principals see these conditions as having some influence. All private sector groups feel that: "demand for basics," "drug use," "declining achievement," "competency testing," and "graduation requirements" will have some influence but much less an influence than public school principals believe.

Men and women principals in the private sector schools generally agree with each other on most influences: 11 of the 17. Except for the "demand for basics," women are of the opinion that the conditions will have a greater influence than men believe. Men and women did not agree concerning the influence of the following conditions: "student nonattendance," "national youth service," "lower compulsory attendance age," "community based learning," "finance and general economy." On these items women feel they would have a stronger influence than the men.

41

Summary

The private sector high school principals, both religious-affiliated and private and both men and women, are experienced, mature, and highly educated with diverse educational backgrounds. They find great satisfaction in their work, and they view outside influences, administrative "road blocks," and legal requirements as less constraining than do their public school counterparts. Men and women principals do not differ much in their views of educational issues, the tasks of secondary education, or in the ways in which they allocate their time on the job. Private sector school principals and public school principals differ markedly in teaching responsibility, scope of authority, independence of action, priorities accorded the tasks of education, views of federal aid to private sector schools. Private sector school principals are much more concerned about finance and the general economy. With the exception of the bi-modal distributions relative to certain characteristics and concerns of private school principals, the picture is a reassuring one. The private sector principals are a competent group and reasonably united in opinions and points of view. They share the interests and concerns of their public school colleagues.

42

4 The Study of Future Forces and Conditions

AN ANALYSIS OF FUTURE FORCES and conditions likely to affect secondary schooling was considered important to a comprehensive study of the principalship. Secondary schools, serving youth in a youth-oriented society, must live with constant social change. These changes should be anticipated whenever possible so that schools can engage in conscious planning rather than reacting hurriedly to new circumstances as they occur. Good planning, based in part upon an awareness of imminent change, can increase the effectiveness of schools.

One irritant to principals is their immersion in a sea of daily details. Seldom do they have the opportunity to look ahead and formulate programs for faculty and students. Past studies of the principalship have not been especially helpful in this regard as they tend to stress the documentation of current and past events, providing a static picture rather than looking toward the future and its requirements.

The investigation of future forces and conditions in this study of the principalship involved analysis of 45 statements covering future conditions in five areas of life: (1) political/legal, (2) economic, (3) social, (4) technological, and (5) institutional/educational. In addition, a request for open-ended responses was included. Respondents were asked to make two projections, a three-to-five year forecast and a 10-year forecast, for each of the statements provided. They were also requested to estimate the potential impact upon secondary education of each circumstance, should it actually occur in the future.

Two groups of persons were asked to respond to the instrument, high school principals and national political leaders. It was felt that each group would possess valid and unique perspectives on future forces and conditions likely to affect education. The principals' group included the 60 effective principals from the Volume II study, while the 28 members of the Advisory Committee to the Congressional Clearinghouse on the Future comprised the national political leadership group. This committee of four senators and 24 members of the House of Representatives are prominent congressmen with a special interest in the future. The Clearinghouse sponsors publications and programs for the benefit of its membership and of federal lawmakers generally.

Usable returns were received from 43 principals, a 71 percent response, and from 14 congressmen or their chiefs of staff, a 50 percent return. Data were organized to determine whether assumptions could be met for chi-square analysis. These requirements were satisfied in only three cases due to the small number of congressmen and their chiefs of staff in the study. The data, therefore, are presented in percentages since usual tests of statistical significance are not appropriate.

The complete futures instrument, including all responses of the two groups, are included as appendices A and B. Analysis of these responses indicated that the most practical and useful data are those coming from the three-to-five year projections. The two appendices include all data, however, for persons interested in opinions beyond those summarized here in the narrative report.

This chapter reports directly on the opinions of the two groups of respondents as they project forces and conditions for three to five years into the future. It suggests that on some issues principals and national political leaders see eye to eye, while on other statements the two groups differ sharply. Each of the five sections of the futures study is reported in sequence, reflecting the organization of the instrument.

Political and Legal Factors

The political/legal arena has been an active force for change during the past decade and continues today to impact upon secondary education. At the national level these conditions include new federal directives, regulatory controls, court decisions, legislative actions, initiatives by advocacy groups, and moves to establish a Department of Education. At the state level, political/legal forces affecting education include legislation and board rulings involving collective bargaining, certification requirements, outcomes accountability, diploma requirements, and the age for compulsory attendance. What is the impact of these and other forces projected to the future?

Principals and national political leaders, as they forecast the political/legal factors likely to affect schools, agree on some projections but disagree on others. The two groups, for example, view the likelihood of continued growth in federal control quite differently. Congressional opinion is evenly divided about the probability of additional federal influence upon schools while principals expect federal growth in education to continue.

		Probability of Occurrence	
		Doubtful/ Possible	Likely/ Certain
Statement			
Federal control of secondary education (i.e., categorical aid programs, civil rights actions, reports on attendance and meals, Title IX, etc.) will grow.	Political Leaders	50%	50%
	Principals	16%	84%

Outlook differs between national leaders and principals on two additional political/legal factors, the establishment of a Department of Education and the extension of efforts toward desegration. For example, all the congressmen polled definitely expect a Department of Education to be formed within three to five years, while a solid 36 percent of the principals doubt that this will occur. Also, principals anticipate new initiatives for desegregation programs while the majority of political leaders do not expect this to occur.

Statement		Probability of Occurrence	
		Doubtful/ Possible	Likely/ Certain
A Department of Education will be established with a cabinet-level secretary.	Political Leaders	0%	100%
	Principals	36%	65%
Desegregation efforts will be expanded in most metropolitan areas.	Political Leaders	61%	39%
	Principals	30%	70%

On a majority of political/legal factors, however, the congressmen and principals agree. They *do not* expect the following conditions to occur within the next three to five years:

- The age of compulsory education to be lowered.
- The schools to lose "educational malpractice" litigation for awarding diplomas to students with deficient skills.
- The collective bargaining rights of teachers to be curtailed.
- The current certification requirements of teachers or administrators to be eliminated.

Political leaders and principals together *do* expect these factors to continue over the next five years:

- A furtherance by courts of the legal rights of children and youth.
- A growth in power of organized teachers' associations.
- The holding of schools as accountable for specific, measurable results.
- The employment of affirmative action programs for job placement and college admissions.

The specific percentages for each statement are reported in appendices "A" and "B."

In summary, then, as national political leaders and principals look at future political/legal forces and conditions likely to affect secondary education, the congressmen tend to anticipate a pause in the growth of federal regulations while principals expect an extension of the heavy federal hand. Neither group forecasts a dramatic change in the direction of recent court decisions or legislation affecting compulsory education, constitutional prerogatives, certification, or personnel actions. Both groups expect that schools will be held accountable for student outcomes or results.

Economic Factors

The advent of rapid inflation, the slow growth of the economy, the rising costs of energy, and the citizen tax revolt are all economic factors that could seriously affect secondary schools during the years ahead. Depending upon the priorities granted to education by the public, schools could be forced by economic conditions to curtail their programs and services. What is the likelihood of these or other economic factors actually affecting schools? Can schools identify and react constructively to emerging economic forces? Can principals anticipate economic conditions to the best advantage of their students and their schools?

The national political leaders tend to be more optimistic than principals about the impact of economic conditions upon schools. They appear confident that schools will not be abandoned to a general tax revolt or the cost of living squeeze.

		Probability of Occurrence	
		Doubtful/ Possible	Likely/ Certain
Statement			
Difficulties in the national economy will force schools to initiate additional budget cuts.	Political Leaders	58%	42%
	Principals	27%	73%
Steps will be taken by federal and/or state governments to end school closures due to underfunding.	Political Leaders	36%	64%
	Principals	76%	24%

The predicted source of financial support for education apparently will shift, however. The congressmen and principals both see increased resistance to the heavy use of property taxes to support local government, including schools. They also agree that "income taxes and sales taxes will replace property taxes as the main source of school revenue."

The national political leaders are more certain than principals are that public funds or tax credits will not be provided for the support of private schools.

		Probability of Occurrence	
		Doubtful/ Possible	Likely/ Certain
Statement			
Financial support will be provided for private schools through tuition tax credits or by direct funding from tax revenues.	Political Leaders	85%	15%
	Principals	68%	32%

Basically, the national political leaders and the principals project an optimistic outlook toward the impact of a tightening economy upon schools. No disasters are anticipated, although the principals tend to be more apprehensive than the congressmen. The revolt against property taxes is expected to be counterbalanced by supplemental revenues from other sources. Neither group expects a major shift toward the public funding of private schools. In short, the projections involve some shifts in the sources of funds, but no dramatic change in the amount of funds available or in the kinds of institutions benefiting from those funds.

Social Factors

Social expectations for schools tend to vary from decade to decade. In 1957, after Sputnik, the citizens wanted schools to focus upon science and mathematics, while by 1967 attention had shifted to student rights, open education, and learning alternatives. As society approaches 1980, new expectations appear to be emerging which may affect schools. Again, the outlook of national political leaders does not coincide with principals on certain of these expectations.

		Possibility of Occurrence	
		Doubtful/ Possible	Likely/ Certain
Statement			
Moral education or values education will become more common in high schools.	Political Leaders	82%	18%
	Principals	48%	52%
Parents and citizens will expect to participate in establishing objectives and priorities for schools.	Political Leaders	8%	92%
	Principals	24%	76%

On most social issues, however, congressmen and principals see eye to eye. For example, both groups agree overwhelmingly that society will *not* become "deschooled." They also agree that business and labor will *not* assume major responsibilities for educating significant numbers of youth aged 16-18.

Neither group sees much immediate assistance for schools in providing social services for students, one of the major new responsibilities assumed by educational institutions over the past decade. By an overwhelming margin the political leaders and principals agree that social functions such as serving breakfasts, providing psychological services, and furnishing jobs will continue to be the responsibility of the school rather than be assumed by nonschool public agencies.

A sharply divided opinion exists within both groups concerning expectations for schools in response to social problems like drug abuse and weakening family structures.

Statement		*Possibility of Occurrence*	
		Doubtful/ Possible	Likely/ Certain
Social indicators such as increase in crime, family breakdown, drug usage, etc., will result in additional new programs for schools.	Political Leaders	46%	54%
	Principals	44%	56%

Finally, about one-third of the national political leaders expect that full employment programs or national service programs will be developed for youth while less than one-fifth of the principals anticipate this development.

The total response of congressmen and of principals to social factors likely to affect schools over the next three to five years is, to some degree, one of uncertainty. On the one hand, strong confidence exists that schools as agencies for educating youth will not be replaced by other institutions; but, on the other hand, little consensus exists about the actual role and responsibilities of schools as social conditions become changed. Do schools develop programs to counteract every social deficiency? Are social problems like family breakdown more appropriately addressed by schools or by other institutions? In fact, can serious social change be affected by schools in any event?

Evidence by Jenks and others suggests that schools are not effective social change agents. The issue of whether or not schools can respond usefully for their students to broad social change appears, therefore, to be an open question. Also open to opinion is the matter of whether or not secondary schools actually have an obligation in this area considering their continuing responsibilities to educate youth. Public indecision about the role of schools amidst rapid social change is, in sum, reflected in the responses found in this "social factors" section of the questionnaire.

Technological Factors

Instructional technology has developed rapidly over the past decade. The electronics industry has assembled an impressive faculty of machines to instruct students, ranging from simple television monitors and audio cassettes to computers with visual displays and sophisticated feedback mechanisms. Does this new technology constitute a revolution in the delivery of instruction or is it rather an interesting but decided supplement to the traditional *homo sapiens* teacher? What is its place during the next five years as students learn in school and elsewhere?

The national political leaders see a greater application of educational technology than do principals.

Statement		Possibility of Occurrence	
		Doubtful/ Possible	Likely/ Certain
Mini-computers, video-discs, and other technology will be widely used in schools	Political Leaders	10%	90%
	Principals	49%	51%
Computer-assisted instruction will become common in schools.	Political Leaders	27%	73%
	Principals	59%	41%

The reluctance of principals to endorse technology strongly probably reflects the difficulties encountered to date with using television and other electronic media in schools. It may also reflect the high cost of computer-assisted instruction. Principals in the 1977 NASSP study of the high school principalship, in fact, rated instructional technology as less promising than did principals in the 1965 study.

Implementing technology has proven difficult. Dial access retrieval mechanisms and language laboratories, for example, become inoperable because of mechanical failures. Some of these failures are caused by students who disassemble the most complex of protective devices or who use gum and glue in ingenious ways. Providing appropriate software also poses a serious problem, causing many schools to cut back on plans for instruction by television. Then, too, a growing body of research indicates that students do not learn as well from electronic media as from human teachers, and that students prefer the social contact of teachers to sitting with machines. Despite these drawbacks a significant percentage of principals remains optimistic that over the long run technology will move toward its promise.

Whatever the ultimate role assumed by technology in the secondary schools of America, one point of agreement is clear between national political figures and principals—only a limited amount of schooling will take place in the home through video and other technologies. Evidently both the congressmen and the principals are skeptical about youth being motivated to learn by technology at home. Both

49

groups also see writing as maintaining its central place in the curriculum. By an overwhelming margin, the congressmen and principals agree that oral and video-based communication will not replace instruction about writing in secondary schools.

Educational Factors

When asked if significant changes are likely to occur in educational practices and expectations for schools, most of the respondents in both groups foresaw no dramatic shift. The national political leaders expect that programs for adults in secondary schools will grow significantly while principals are divided on this question. For the most part, however, all respondents tended to predict extensions of current directions rather than dramatic new thrusts.

		Possibility of Occurrence	
		Doubtful/ Possible	Likely/ Certain
Statement			
Schools will become more "basic," cutting back on individual options and alternatives.	Political Leaders	27%	73%
	Principals	35%	65%
The senior year of high school will disappear.	Political Leaders	100%	0%
	Principals	97%	3%
National standards for the high school diploma will be established.	Political Leaders	80%	20%
	Principals	89%	11%
Competency-based certification for teachers and administrators will become common.	Political Leaders	73%	27%
	Principals	82%	18%
Student interscholastic athletics will be replaced by club teams sponsored by community groups.	Political Leaders	100%	0%
	Principals	98%	2%

50

Neither group expects teacher tenure to be severely curtailed or abolished over the next three to five years, or that federal funds will be distributed to support "parenting education," or that the diploma will be "established as a certificate of guarantee of basic skills," or that early graduation will disappear.

While agreement generally exists between congressmen and principals that the enrollment decline will affect private and public schools alike, a significant percentage of these national leaders expects that private schools will maintain or increase their enrollments in the years ahead.

Statement		*Possibility of Occurrence*	
		Doubtful/ Possible	Likely/ Certain
Private secondary schools will maintain or increase their enrollment as public school enrollment drops.	Political Leaders	64%	36%
	Principals	76%	24%

On the matter of test scores, the national political leaders and principals see good news ahead. Both groups expect that test scores will not continue to decline as has been the tendency over the past decade.

Taken overall, the principals tend to be slightly more cautious than congressmen about expected institutional change. While agreement exists generally, the principals see a smaller shift in school functions and requirements than do members of congress. Fewer principals expect a trend toward the basics, fewer see a loss of enrollment to private schools, fewer anticipate national standards for the high school diploma to develop, and fewer expect to see competency-based certification for professionals.

It is interesting to observe that on political and social factors, however, the opposite picture prevails. Principals tend to see greater movement in the economic and political world than do national political leaders. More principals than congressmen expect to see new activity in civil rights, additional federal control of education, more severe economic conditions, and a cutback in property taxes. Perhaps the responses substantiate the old adage that people tend to be more cautious in their own field than when conjecturing about other occupations.

Ten-Year Projections

Respondents were asked to make 10-year projections of change as well as projections of three to five years. Because long-term estimates tend to be unstable, these opinions are not reported in detail here. They are, however, fully documented in appendices "A" and "B."

Taken together, the long-range projections tend to reflect the direction of the shorter projections. For example, 64 percent of the principals consider it likely or certain that a Department of Education will be established in three to five years, while 72 percent of principals expect a Department of Education within 10 years.

A few exceptions exist to this general rule. For example:

1. A majority of congressmen agree that in 10 years difficulties with the national economy will force budget cuts.

2. A majority of congressmen expect that in 10 years financial support will be provided for private schools through tuition tax credits or by tax revenues.

3. A majority of congressmen expect that in 10 years a concern for "quality of life" or "smaller is better" will cause major changes in the curriculum.

4. A near consensus exists among principals that in 10 years social problems, such as family breakdown, will result in new programs for schools.

5. Almost half of the congressmen and the principals expect that in 10 years the social service functions assigned to schools, such as serving breakfasts, will be assumed by other agencies.

6. About half of the principals anticipate that in 10 years the diploma will be established as a certificate of basic skills, and that the competency-based certification of teachers and administrators will become common.

Open Response Questions

The questionnaire on future forces and conditions included space for open comments by the respondents. Only about half of the principals and less than one quarter of the national political leaders gave additional views in the space provided. Most frequently their observations about future forces and conditions likely to affect secondary education focused upon these topics:

1. The decline in enrollment

2. The accountability "movement"

3. A move toward basic or traditional education

4. The prospect of new medical discoveries and new energy sources

5. The extension of education to encompass additional community agencies

6. The growth of continuing or adult education

7. New attempts to individualize education through methodology or computers or both.

None of these conditions were predicted by more than four persons.

In summary, no striking consensus or dramatic predictions about future forces were found in the open-ended section of the futures questionnaire.

Implications for Schools

The future is difficult to predict, as evidenced by such surprises as the Arab oil embargo of 1973. Futurists less than a decade ago were projecting a 30-hour work week and an embarrassing surplus of funds in the national treasury. Both of these promises have evaporated with a growing trade deficit, tougher international economic competition, and dwindling natural resources.

In education, as in the economy, the unanticipated frequently occurs. Who would have predicted in 1972 or 1973 the current interest in basic skills or in competency testing? Who would have predicted the advent of Proposition 13 and similar severe constraints upon property tax support for schools? Who would have anticipated the comprehensive requirements of Public Law 94-142?

Planning for the future always involves a mixture of knowns and unknowns, leavened by some educated guesses. Schools obviously cannot anticipate all unexpected events or surprising conditions that will occur. But schools can assume a forward posture, an awareness of emerging trends in the economy and in the public mind. Anticipating these trends and then posturing the school appropriately may make the difference between controlled, effective change, and nerve-shattering crises.

This study of future forces and conditions likely to affect schools presents some knowns together with some educated guesses. The unknowns must come from man's unfolding history. The knowns provide important clues to planning, however. They offer two or three steps up the ladder of the future. They help anticipate its requirements.

Based upon the opinions of the national political leaders and principals as expressed in this study, certain useful generalizations can be made about future conditions affecting secondary schools:

- First, the picture is generally optimistic. Schools will survive; adequate funding will be provided and youth will continue to be educated by schools rather than by replacement institutions. Compulsory education will remain a national commitment. Professional certification will continue as a requirement for teaching and administration.

- A Department of Education will be established but federal intrusion upon local and state prerogatives may be alleviated. These events are not contradictory. The majority of national political leaders do not anticipate the continued expansion of federal regulations and directives affecting schooling. A Department of Education will likely focus its attention upon educational matters rather than upon broad social concerns.

- Schools will be expected to identify and document the outcomes of education. While basic cognitive skills currently enjoy a high priority, the concept of making schools accountable for results may extend to broader educational objectives as well.

- The redefinition of constitutional rights will continue for students, for teachers, and for minorities.

53

- A cutback in property taxes will be replaced by sales and income taxes within the states, and possibly by federal revenues.

- Private schools will compete with public schools for the smaller pool of students entering secondary education.

- Expectations will continue for schools to adjust their curriculum to meet the requirements of social change, such as family difficulties or economic imperatives. Schools, however, may receive assistance from other institutions to provide social services to youth.

- The application of technology to instruction will be gradual and evolutionary rather than sudden and dramatic. Teachers will remain central to the instructional process.

- No major institutional changes are anticipated. The twelfth grade will not disappear, interscholastic athletics will thrive, teacher tenure will prevail, and standards for the high school diploma will continue to be established by state and local governments.

Considered broadly, the secondary schools will continue to change into the immediate future and this change can be taken to account in school planning. But these modifications will be evolutionary, not revolutionary in character.

5 The Future Principal

THE THREE MAJOR INVESTIGATIONS and the auxiliary inquiries which constitute the National Study of the High School Principalship provide no singular, conclusive profile of today's principal. Some strong outlines are evident, but the position is flexible. Job demands vary from site to site; thus skill requirements differ from role to role. The principal is much more than an administrative automaton trained for a series of interchangeable slots. Those who attain success in the principalship are able, adaptable individuals who can function in an evolving role. They know how to "read" their institutions and communities with clarity and they act with assurance.

A person's interactions with job demands and the conditions of a particular setting create unique challenges and opportunities. This uniqueness does not mean that commonalities don't exist or that generalizations cannot be made. Rather, it suggests that attempts to project the principalship into the future must recognize important limitations. These include the normal strictures of prediction as well as the tolerances required for applying generalizations to specific cases.

The investigators believe, therefore, that the most useful projections come from an analysis of directions which are indicated by the data and appear to be most in need of attention. These directions are selected because certain trends are already established and well recognized; some are reasonably documented from the futures study, some are apparent from the conditions reported by principals and "significant others," and some emerged as circumstances which obviously will require attention in the course of time.

Implications for the future principal are considered under three topics: external conditions, personal-professional factors, and the school and the principalship. This section concludes with a profile of the future principal.

External Conditions and Expectations

Conditions expected to face principals in the future are summarized in the preceding chapter. In one sense the outlook appears diffi-

55

cult, with forecasts indicating a shifting (and perhaps diminishing) tax base, demands for documenting student outcomes, and expectations that new curricula must be developed to meet emerging social problems. But from another view the picture looks encouraging, with schools receiving solid endorsement as the central educational institution for youth, with expectations that new technologies and methodologies be tried, and with anticipation that institutional change will be gradual rather than abrupt.

These forces and others identified in the futures study, such as declining enrollment, could generate state or federal legislation or legal decisions and court orders which would alter the responsibilities of principals. Some of these actions might modify the job tasks required or affect the relationship of principals to staff, students, and community. If this occurs, narrow administrative responses will prove inadequate to minimizing conflict and to assuring educational quality.

Three external forces appear especially likely to affect secondary school principals in the future regardless of economic conditions. These are:

- Expectations by the public to participate in setting objectives for schools and to receive reports of progress on reaching those objectives;

- An overall decline in enrollment of 15 percent; and

- The advent of new methodology, technology, and courses arising from research and from social demands.

All indicators point to a continued strong citizen presence in schools. This presence ranges from policy formulation by appointed groups to the enrollment of individual adults in courses of study. Public participation is shifting from one of reacting to events to one of helping to determine expectations. Viewed as "educational consumerism," it reflects a well established trend in American society. This trend does not necessarily indicate additional public interference in school affairs, but rather it points toward a different kind of participation with less attention to individual problems and more attention to collective expectations. For the principal, this participation suggests the importance of formulating annual school plans which utilize needs assessment, include a consideration of community priorities, and provide clear reporting systems.

Enrollment decline extends beyond the serious matter of school closings and budget reductions. It also may force cutbacks in the curriculum, cause the evolution of an older faculty, and require a reappraisal of administrative staffing. The downsizing of a school places heavy planning and staffing burdens upon the principal. It also requires close liaison with parents and community.

Reductions in school size do not mean that a freeze occurs in courses and methodologies. Expectations that schools respond to new technologies and to changing social conditions will continue. Attempts to define and operationalize individualized education (as expressed by the IEP required by Public Law 94-142), plans for new courses suggested by new social problems, and the appearance of less costly technology will all make their impact upon secondary schools during the 1980s.

External conditions will not submerge principals as the future unfolds, but these conditions do require an alert, well prepared, and energetic response to direct these conditions into constructive channels. The key will be to manage change so that students will achieve the expected outcomes, within a system that must operate from a reduced size and resource base. This may appear to be a difficult act, but it will be aided by a renewed public commitment to secondary schools and their unique mission, and with the likelihood of reduced federal interference.

Personal/Professional Factors

The views of principals on broad educational issues shifted dramatically from 1965 to 1977, reflecting a serious concern for social conditions and for the school's role in resolving them. The principals, when considering educational goals, however, shifted their views only slightly, giving a higher priority to learner self-concept and a lower priority to teaching moral and spiritual values. Principals evidently view educational objectives as relatively unchanging but see institutional arrangements and climates for achieving them as changing with society. This solid agreement suggests that principals reflect a social awareness while holding to established values for education.

Indications are that personal characteristics, professional preparation, and career routes to the principalship will continue along the trends shown between 1965 and 1977. Principals are slightly older now than in 1965, have spent more time in their current posts, have completed more formal preparation, are more active in their professional associations, and have arrived at the principalship through the assistant principalship. Despite declining enrollments, the high school is a large, complex organization which will continue to require leaders with advanced preparation, experience, maturity, human sensitivity, and intelligent assessment of social/political climates and their educational implications. The data imply that these attributes of the principalship have been enhanced during the past decade by training and experience.

The High School and the Principalship

Dominant factors in the evolution of high schools over the past decade are increases in both size and expenditure levels. Neither trend will continue into the future. The large high school (2,500 and above) is not viewed as desirable—no principal in the entire survey indicated an optimal size above 2,500 students and only four percent selected 2,000 to 2,500 students as preferable. Budget restrictions are anticipated, as well. In the futures study, only 41 percent of the national political leaders indicated that additional budget cutting will occur in the three-to-five-year time frame, but 76 percent indicate such cuts within 10 years. The effective principals' group is even more certain of budget cuts causing a serious impact upon secondary schools if predictions prevail.

The comprehensive high school has increased in popularity over other types of high schools since 1965 as have "alternative" schools, the only other category showing growth. Some opinion exists, however, that the impending enrollment decline will affect public schools more than private schools. Few persons expect new growth in alternative forms of schooling and most see a limited impact from the new technologies. Neither principals nor citizens expect schooling to take place in the home, nor do they anticipate that business/industry/labor will take on more educational responsibilities.

Economic retrenchment and smaller enrollments will not mean a less complex or demanding job for the principal. The evidence indicates complications and new problems across the board. On the bright side, schools are not likely to receive cuts in categorical funds for special programs. Moreover, the pressures for more adult programs will provide opportunities to educate the public about school needs as well as to give them the educational opportunities they seek. Outside evidence, especially public opinions polls, indicates solid support for public education and a desire to see school budgets as the last to be cut. This reservoir of good will can be widened.

A most compelling force is the involvement of school with community. Planning skills are basic to a successful involvement of community groups. The principal will continue to be challenged as well by the power of professional organizations, including actions involving collective bargaining and associated teacher organization activities. Problems and dilemmas can, therefore, be expected in the areas of public and professional involvement.

The principalship may be enhanced by the movement to provide more autonomy and accountability for the local school. This movement is still forming and will be further experimented with during the next decade as certain models and exemplars appear. Within this framework, program and staff evaluation, already mentioned as areas of recognized weakness, appear to be crucial. Professional associations and universities will need to give attention to these two areas if principals are to be served adequately.

The Principal's Job

The forces and conditions expected to unfold do not offer much hope that one of the most pressing problems of the principalship, time demands and time management, will be alleviated. Principals report frustration in controlling their time allocations. This will persist into the future. A fundamental challenge for the next decade will be that of reconstructing the principalship so that job tasks are controlled in an effective and rewarding way.

The increased complexity of schools requires that the principal assume new management tasks. Time-demand problems, noted above, are largely caused by a serious management overload. Severe managerial problems began with the dramatic increase in school size which occurred between 1965 and 1977. (In 1965, 65 percent of the high schools had enrollments under 500; in 1967 this percentage dropped to 23.8, and the number of schools with over 2,000 students doubled.) An overload in such matters as supervision and discipline resulted from this growth. Meanwhile, new demands came from parents, teachers, and students for accessibility to the principal. To continue this brief scenario, externally imposed requirements such as due process, accountability, union contracts, mandated programs, and similar demands added to the management overload.

During the 1980s initiatives to create new administrative structures will be taken to enable the principal to shed routine tasks and to focus upon the central mission of the school. The exact directions are indefinite but awareness of the problem is growing along with a realization of the importance of the principal's leadership to educational quality. Some new arrangements for allowing improved accessibility will be implemented. "No nonsense" delegation and techniques of sharing responsibility are among approaches likely to come. New consideration will be given to the autonomy accorded to principals by the district office. Decentralization of management is a strong trend in the private sector.

Within the school the job of the principal will become more outcomes oriented and less concerned with process and procedures. The administrative team framework will be extended to program development and staff supervision.

Management techniques will become more regularized; that is, more widely adopted in a standardized format so that the procedures, and even the data derived from them, will be compatible from school to school. Among these techniques are an annual planning effort resulting from needs assessment and the identification and prioritizing of

59

goals, budget determination based upon this planning, and program development and evaluation systems with feedback for monitoring progress. This does not imply a rigid control mechanism but rather a more clearly specified set of procedures so that administrators are freed from daily management tasks and the constant supervision of routine activities and functions.

Preparation and Selection of Principals

The education and selection of principals today is uncoordinated, perhaps even casual. Studies show that among institutions of higher education there is a wide variety in selection criteria and professional courses for the principalship. Certification requirements also differ from state to state. Job placement often ignores the need to match particular capabilities to particular job requirements.

The best talent available must be encouraged to prepare for and assume the principalship. Sufficient knowledge exists about the skills required for success in the principalship to do better at identifying and placing promising persons than now ordinarily occurs. Successful principals apply problem analysis to determine the important elements of a situation, use good judgment in identifying educational needs, perceive differences in requirements and expectations, and are decisive as required. They also communicate clearly with a variety of audiences, plan and organize well, and possess strong interpersonal skills—they are tactful, sensitive, emotionally stable, and encourage confidence. They also are highly motivated and sufficiently flexible to respond to change.

Added to these traits and skills must be adequate professional knowledge, beginning with an understanding of leadership, curriculum development, school law, school management, human relations, and community composition. This knowledge needs to be applied—and extended—in an internship experience. In sum, the ability to work with people, together with the application of professional knowledge will make the successful principal of the future. These competencies should be diagnosed during the preservice process and provided for if missing.

Finally, their presence should be verified by the employing school district prior to job placement. The use of assessment centers is one technique to accomplish this goal.

Profile of the Future Principal

To conclude this volume the authors wish to make observations about the future principal and his needs as a professional person. With the evidence of the national study and related work in mind, comment is offered about capabilities which appear to be essential to effective principals of the future. The points listed below encompass 11 essential attributes.

60

Characteristics and early preparation. Effective principals exhibit definite personal qualities. They are unthreatened and optimistic, open and outgoing, secure and confident, active and energetic, understanding and tolerant. This is not a wish-list of traits. Schools are human institutions in which interpersonal conflict can be expected, in which activities are varied and often hectic, and in which young people and staff need a secure and confident, as well as outgoing, administrative leader with a high tolerance for frustration and a high level of energy.

In addition, schools are educational institutions and those who lead them must be educated individuals in the best sense of that term. Adequate evidence exists to support the view that, regardless of the major focus of academic preparation and teaching experience, significant amounts of study are needed in the social sciences—significant in the sense of obtaining a perspective about the evolution of social movements, a grasp of political and economic forces, and an understanding of important ideas and events. Selection and recruitment into administration of individuals who exemplify this type of background represents a major task for education.

Experience leading to the principalship. Successful teaching experience, advanced degree study in educational administration (including an internship), and administrative experience, particularly in a challenging assistant principalship, are indicated by the study data as almost universal for the effective principals. These experiences and attendant formal study should build expertise in the next three areas.

Knowledge and experience with educational programs. The principal must have adequate knowledge of and experience with the variety of educational programs and program proposals found in the modern high school. He should know how to design a program, write program specifications, and conduct program/curriculum development activities. Above all he must be able to present intelligently and defend both the overall school program and specific elements which compose it.

Management skills. A configuration of management skills are described in the preceding section. These seem to represent the minimum essential management tools for the effective principal of the future. However, the principal must not only know these in the technical sense, he must also know them in the analytical sense—what each tool can and cannot provide, the uses and limitations of information generated, etc. As indicated earlier, management skills aim at outcomes but they should not do so in any narrow, mechanistic way.

Leadership skills. This term has unfortunately become a "catchall" for a set of vaguely defined and imprecise activities. What the evidence relative to principals indicates is that the effective principal knows how to work with a variety of people to get *commitment* for educational programs, ideas, and activities. He can solve the human problems at-

61

tendant to getting "on task" and to do so he employs communication skills of all kinds including listening, clarifying, and summarizing, but perhaps most of all he perceives every encounter and communication opportunity as an avenue to educate others and he does so with a soft hand.

Staffing. A critical factor in effectiveness is staffing practices—selection, supervision, evaluation, and development. Every principal will be faced with the leadership of an administrative and professional staff. No principal can avoid the staff responsibilities noted without suffering loss of effectiveness.

Reading community expectations and interpreting social movement. Today's "publics" insist upon participating in many aspects of education to include secondary schools. They can be a valuable resource. Futures data indicate increased participation in setting goals and priorities, policy making, and even resource allocation. In addition, interest groups will surely continue to pressure for special consideration. The effective principal must be perceptive. He must "read" his community, interpret social movements in educational terms, and find ways to use community energies for the best interests of education.

Educational perspective and future orientation. High schools can no longer lag behind their communities and the wider society. The principal needs the perspectives alluded to above and the planning skills to project into the future. The importance of annual planning has been mentioned, but also required are the skills to involve staff in long and short-range planning.

Continued professional development. Effective principals showed an active interest and participation in career planning and in personal and professional growth. As a group they were more active in professional associations, had more advanced formal training, read more, and managed their careers more deliberately than do principals generally. All principals indicated they needed to put more time in this area than they currently are. Beyond this, the principal leads an educational institution committed to unending, continued learning; and the job itself will soon make obsolete the individual who does not continue professional and personal growth.

School autonomy. Principals should expect schools to become more independent from day-by-day control by the district office. Management trends indicate local units will be given target objectives and then provided with considerable autonomy in reaching those objectives. This gives principals new discretion to act, but also new requirements to plan, to operate, and to account for the results.

The principal as educator. The configuration of attributes described above add up to an image of the principal as educator. But the parts do not in themselves constitute the whole. The administrator must see himself as an educator and seek to fulfill that ultimate role. At a practical level the principal must know the difference between good and poor learning situations, recognize well directed and misdirected instruction, understand what is required technically to alter conditions, and be able to project the essential components necessary to achieve a sound education for every student. He must *know* and he also must *care.*

Appendix A

I. Political and Legal Factors   Principals

(All figures are percentages)

1. A Department of Education will be established with a cabinet-level secretary.

Yrs.	PROBABILITY OF OCCURRENCE				POTENTIAL FOR IMPACT ON SECONDARY SCHOOLS			
	Doubtful	Possible	Likely	Certain	None	Marginal	Moderate	Strong
3-5	12	24	55	9	2	31	43	24
10	14	14	40	32	7	14	50	29

2. Federal control of secondary education (i.e., categorical aid programs, civil rights actions, reports on attendance and meals, Title IX, etc.) will grow.

Yrs.	PROBABILITY OF OCCURRENCE				POTENTIAL FOR IMPACT ON SECONDARY SCHOOLS			
	Doubtful	Possible	Likely	Certain	None	Marginal	Moderate	Strong
3-5	2	14	56	28	2	9	40	49
10	7	23	33	37	3	10	37	50

3. Desegregation efforts will be expanded in most metropolitan areas.

Yrs.	PROBABILITY OF OCCURRENCE				POTENTIAL FOR IMPACT ON SECONDARY SCHOOLS			
	Doubtful	Possible	Likely	Certain	None	Marginal	Moderate	Strong
3-5	12	18	50	20	5	8	52	35
10	18	22	30	30	0	24	40	36

4. Affirmative action programs will remain a central factor in job placement and college admissions.

Yrs.	PROBABILITY OF OCCURRENCE				POTENTIAL FOR IMPACT ON SECONDARY SCHOOLS			
	Doubtful	Possible	Likely	Certain	None	Marginal	Moderate	Strong
3-5	5	12	56	27	3	17	56	24
10	6	25	50	19	3	33	54	10

5. The courts will assert further the rights of children and youth.

Yrs.	PROBABILITY OF OCCURRENCE				POTENTIAL FOR IMPACT ON SECONDARY SCHOOLS			
	Doubtful	Possible	Likely	Certain	None	Marginal	Moderate	Strong
3-5	20	20	48	12	5	25	45	25
10	17	30	33	20	0	31	38	31

6. Organized teacher associations will become more powerful at the state and national levels.

Yrs.	PROBABILITY OF OCCURRENCE				POTENTIAL FOR IMPACT ON SECONDARY SCHOOLS			
	Doubtful	Possible	Likely	Certain	None	Marginal	Moderate	Strong
3-5	5	19	38	38	0	5	26	69
10	10	10	37	43	0	3	30	67

7. States will limit or eliminate the current education requirements for certification of teachers and school administrators.

Yrs.	PROBABILITY OF OCCURRENCE				POTENTIAL FOR IMPACT ON SECONDARY SCHOOLS			
	Doubtful	Possible	Likely	Certain	None	Marginal	Moderate	Strong
3-5	81	12	7	0	17	53	20	10
10	44	38	9	9	10	35	32	23

8. The age for compulsory education will be lowered in most states.

Yrs.	PROBABILITY OF OCCURRENCE				POTENTIAL FOR IMPACT ON SECONDARY SCHOOLS			
	Doubtful	Possible	Likely	Certain	None	Marginal	Moderate	Strong
3-5	58	32	10	0	13	51	21	15
10	41	38	12	9	9	29	33	29

9. Schools will be held accountable for specific, measurable results.

Yrs.	PROBABILITY OF OCCURRENCE				POTENTIAL FOR IMPACT ON SECONDARY SCHOOLS			
	Doubtful	Possible	Likely	Certain	None	Marginal	Moderate	Strong
3-5	2	19	62	17	0	15	32	53
10	0	19	39	42	0	6	21	73

10. Schools will lose "educational malpractice" litigation for awarding diplomas to students with insufficient skills.

Yrs.	PROBABILITY OF OCCURRENCE				POTENTIAL FOR IMPACT ON SECONDARY SCHOOLS			
	Doubtful	Possible	Likely	Certain	None	Marginal	Moderate	Strong
3-5	39	42	17	2	12	30	28	30
10	34	50	16	0	6	34	30	30

11. Legislation will be enacted to curtail collective bargaining rights for public school teachers.

Yrs.	PROBABILITY OF OCCURRENCE				POTENTIAL FOR IMPACT ON SECONDARY SCHOOLS			
	Doubtful	Possible	Likely	Certain	None	Marginal	Moderate	Strong
3-5	62	28	8	2	16	32	39	13
10	32	50	12	6	8	17	46	29

II. Economic Factors

1. Difficulties in the national economy will force schools to initiate additional budget cuts.

	PROBABILITY OF OCCURRENCE				POTENTIAL FOR IMPACT ON SECONDARY SCHOOLS			
Yrs.	Doubtful	Possible	Likely	Certain	None	Marginal	Moderate	Strong
3-5	0	27	46	27	0	5	37	58
10	3	13	42	42	0	3	32	65

2. Resistance will increase to the heavy use of property taxes to support local government, including schools.

	PROBABILITY OF OCCURRENCE				POTENTIAL FOR IMPACT ON SECONDARY SCHOOLS			
Yrs.	Doubtful	Possible	Likely	Certain	None	Marginal	Moderate	Strong
3-5	0	7	40	53	0	0	29	71
10	0	3	26	71	0	0	21	79

3. Income taxes and sales taxes will replace property taxes as the main source of school revenue.

	PROBABILITY OF OCCURRENCE				POTENTIAL FOR IMPACT ON SECONDARY SCHOOLS			
Yrs.	Doubtful	Possible	Likely	Certain	None	Marginal	Moderate	Strong
3-5	22	27	46	5	5	31	41	23
10	0	27	64	9	0	18	46	36

4. Financial support will be provided for private schools through tuition tax credits or by direct funding from tax revenues.

	PROBABILITY OF OCCURRENCE				POTENTIAL FOR IMPACT ON SECONDARY SCHOOLS			
Yrs.	Doubtful	Possible	Likely	Certain	None	Marginal	Moderate	Strong
3-5	40	28	30	2	12	17	38	33
10	13	40	34	13	6	22	38	34

5. Supplementary funding for special students (mentally handicapped, emotionally disturbed, etc.) will be cut back.

	PROBABILITY OF OCCURRENCE				POTENTIAL FOR IMPACT ON SECONDARY SCHOOLS			
Yrs.	Doubtful	Possible	Likely	Certain	None	Marginal	Moderate	Strong
3-5	72	19	9	0	9	28	40	23
10	31	53	16	0	9	16	56	19

6. Steps will be taken by federal and/or state governments to end school closures due to underfunding.

	PROBABILITY OF OCCURRENCE				POTENTIAL FOR IMPACT ON SECONDARY SCHOOLS			
Yrs.	Doubtful	Possible	Likely	Certain	None	Marginal	Moderate	Strong
3-5	39	37	24	0	2	38	48	12
10	10	42	42	6	0	30	38	32

7. Parents will be expected to purchase books and school supplies in the future.

	PROBABILITY OF OCCURRENCE				POTENTIAL FOR IMPACT ON SECONDARY SCHOOLS			
Yrs.	Doubtful	Possible	Likely	Certain	None	Marginal	Moderate	Strong
3-5	64	17	17	2	20	45	33	2
10	43	36	15	6	18	41	35	6

III. Social Factors

1. Society will become "deschooled" with most students learning in community settings.

	PROBABILITY OF OCCURRENCE				POTENTIAL FOR IMPACT ON SECONDARY SCHOOLS			
Yrs.	Doubtful	Possible	Likely	Certain	None	Marginal	Moderate	Strong
3-5	71	26	3	0	24	29	31	16
10	53	42	5	0	19	31	17	33

2. Concern for "quality-of-life" and "small-is-necessary" will foster major changes in the school's curriculum.

	PROBABILITY OF OCCURRENCE				POTENTIAL FOR IMPACT ON SECONDARY SCHOOLS			
Yrs.	Doubtful	Possible	Likely	Certain	None	Marginal	Moderate	Strong
3-5	21	59	15	5	5	45	42	8
10	14	52	20	14	2	44	27	27

3. Full employment and/or national service programs will be developed for youth.

	PROBABILITY OF OCCURRENCE				POTENTIAL FOR IMPACT ON SECONDARY SCHOOLS			
Yrs.	Doubtful	Possible	Likely	Certain	None	Marginal	Moderate	Strong
3-5	23	59	15	3	5	45	39	11
10	17	40	37	6	0	47	35	18

4. Business, industry, and labor will assume responsibilities for educating significant numbers of adolescents aged 16-18.

	PROBABILITY OF OCCURRENCE				POTENTIAL FOR IMPACT ON SECONDARY SCHOOLS			
Yrs.	Doubtful	Possible	Likely	Certain	None	Marginal	Moderate	Strong
3-5	56	31	13	0	16	30	32	22
10	26	51	23	0	0	31	46	23

III. Social Factors *(continued)*

5. Parents and citizens will expect to participate in establishing objectives and priorities for schools.

Yrs.	PROBABILITY OF OCCURRENCE				POTENTIAL FOR IMPACT ON SECONDARY SCHOOLS			
	Doubtful	Possible	Likely	Certain	None	Marginal	Moderate	Strong
3-5	2	22	54	22	2	12	59	27
10	0	13	32	55	0	13	50	37

6. "Social indicators" such as increase in crime, family breakdown, drug usage, etc. will result in additional new programs for schools.

Yrs.	PROBABILITY OF OCCURRENCE				POTENTIAL FOR IMPACT ON SECONDARY SCHOOLS			
	Doubtful	Possible	Likely	Certain	None	Marginal	Moderate	Strong
3-5	7	37	51	5	2	22	59	17
10	0	13	67	20	3	10	60	27

7. Social service functions such as serving breakfasts, providing psychological services, furnishing jobs, etc. will be assumed increasingly by nonschool agencies.

Yrs.	PROBABILITY OF OCCURRENCE				POTENTIAL FOR IMPACT ON SECONDARY SCHOOLS			
	Doubtful	Possible	Likely	Certain	None	Marginal	Moderate	Strong
3-5	55	25	15	5	21	39	32	8
10	9	47	31	13	6	33	49	12

8. Moral education or values education will become more common in high schools.

Yrs.	PROBABILITY OF OCCURRENCE				POTENTIAL FOR IMPACT ON SECONDARY SCHOOLS			
	Doubtful	Possible	Likely	Certain	None	Marginal	Moderate	Strong
3-5	18	30	45	7	3	41	41	15
10	9	28	41	22	3	27	52	18

9. Parents and society will grant youth aged 14-18 additional freedom in the future.

Yrs.	PROBABILITY OF OCCURRENCE				POTENTIAL FOR IMPACT ON SECONDARY SCHOOLS			
	Doubtful	Possible	Likely	Certain	None	Marginal	Moderate	Strong
3-5	47	29	24	0	13	38	27	22
10	35	38	21	6	9	37	30	24

IV. Technological Factors

1. Mini-computers, video-discs, and other technology will be widely used in schools.

Yrs.	PROBABILITY OF OCCURRENCE				POTENTIAL FOR IMPACT ON SECONDARY SCHOOLS			
	Doubtful	Possible	Likely	Certain	None	Marginal	Moderate	Strong
3-5	18	31	38	13	5	28	57	10
10	3	10	52	35	0	10	68	22

2. Much schooling will take place in the home through video and other new technologies.

Yrs.	PROBABILITY OF OCCURRENCE				POTENTIAL FOR IMPACT ON SECONDARY SCHOOLS			
	Doubtful	Possible	Likely	Certain	None	Marginal	Moderate	Strong
3-5	56	38	3	3	20	50	22	8
10	29	54	14	3	9	35	38	18

3. Drugs to control antisocial behavior and to improve mental performance will become common.

Yrs.	PROBABILITY OF OCCURRENCE				POTENTIAL FOR IMPACT ON SECONDARY SCHOOLS			
	Doubtful	Possible	Likely	Certain	None	Marginal	Moderate	Strong
3-5	62	30	8	0	28	45	19	8
10	31	61	8	0	14	55	17	14

4. Computer-assisted instruction will become common in schools.

Yrs.	PROBABILITY OF OCCURRENCE				POTENTIAL FOR IMPACT ON SECONDARY SCHOOLS			
	Doubtful	Possible	Likely	Certain	None	Marginal	Moderate	Strong
3-5	28	31	36	5	11	18	63	8
10	0	35	38	27	0	17	60	23

5. Instruction in oral and video-based communication will largely replace instruction about writing in secondary schools.

Yrs.	PROBABILITY OF OCCURRENCE				POTENTIAL FOR IMPACT ON SECONDARY SCHOOLS			
	Doubtful	Possible	Likely	Certain	None	Marginal	Moderate	Strong
3-5	73	22	5	0	36	33	20	11
10	56	39	5	0	20	38	31	11

V. Institutional Factors

1. Programs for adults in secondary schools will grow significantly.

	PROBABILITY OF OCCURRENCE				POTENTIAL FOR IMPACT ON SECONDARY SCHOOLS			
Yrs.	Doubtful	Possible	Likely	Certain	None	Marginal	Moderate	Strong
3-5	7	48	35	10	10	25	58	7
10	3	23	46	28	3	14	57	26

2. Schools will become more "basic," cutting back on individual options and alternatives.

	PROBABILITY OF OCCURRENCE				POTENTIAL FOR IMPACT ON SECONDARY SCHOOLS			
Yrs.	Doubtful	Possible	Likely	Certain	None	Marginal	Moderate	Strong
3-5	9	26	49	16	2	15	37	46
10	16	23	42	19	0	13	48	39

3. Federal funds will be distributed to support "parenting education."

	PROBABILITY OF OCCURRENCE				POTENTIAL FOR IMPACT ON SECONDARY SCHOOLS			
Yrs.	Doubtful	Possible	Likely	Certain	None	Marginal	Moderate	Strong
3-5	17	49	29	5	12	32	51	5
10	6	27	52	15	3	24	61	12

4. Test scores will continue to drop.

	PROBABILITY OF OCCURRENCE				POTENTIAL FOR IMPACT ON SECONDARY SCHOOLS			
Yrs.	Doubtful	Possible	Likely	Certain	None	Marginal	Moderate	Strong
3-5	42	40	16	2	7	24	49	20
10	63	30	7	0	7	32	45	16

5. The senior year of high school will disappear.

	PROBABILITY OF OCCURRENCE				POTENTIAL FOR IMPACT ON SECONDARY SCHOOLS			
Yrs.	Doubtful	Possible	Likely	Certain	None	Marginal	Moderate	Strong
3-5	77	20	3	0	28	24	24	24
10	46	46	8	0	18	18	18	46

6. Private secondary schools will maintain or increase their enrollment as public school enrollment drops.

	PROBABILITY OF OCCURRENCE				POTENTIAL FOR IMPACT ON SECONDARY SCHOOLS			
Yrs.	Doubtful	Possible	Likely	Certain	None	Marginal	Moderate	Strong
3-5	33	43	19	5	17	26	34	23
10	42	25	28	5	8	30	32	30

7. National standards for the high school diploma will be established.

	PROBABILITY OF OCCURRENCE				POTENTIAL FOR IMPACT ON SECONDARY SCHOOLS			
Yrs.	Doubtful	Possible	Likely	Certain	None	Marginal	Moderate	Strong
3-5	55	34	11	0	27	22	22	29
10	30	46	19	5	14	14	36	36

8. The diploma will be established as a certificate of guarantee of basic skills.

	PROBABILITY OF OCCURRENCE				POTENTIAL FOR IMPACT ON SECONDARY SCHOOLS			
Yrs.	Doubtful	Possible	Likely	Certain	None	Marginal	Moderate	Strong
3-5	33	43	17	7	12	23	35	30
10	9	40	40	11	3	14	43	40

9. Early graduation and other forms of early school leaving will diminish.

	PROBABILITY OF OCCURRENCE				POTENTIAL FOR IMPACT ON SECONDARY SCHOOLS			
Yrs.	Doubtful	Possible	Likely	Certain	None	Marginal	Moderate	Strong
3-5	71	17	10	2	17	58	23	2
10	56	26	15	3	18	52	27	3

10. Teacher tenure will be severely curtailed or abolished in many states.

	PROBABILITY OF OCCURRENCE				POTENTIAL FOR IMPACT ON SECONDARY SCHOOLS			
Yrs.	Doubtful	Possible	Likely	Certain	None	Marginal	Moderate	Strong
3-5	49	38	10	3	21	41	28	10
10	16	51	27	6	6	30	32	32

11. Competency-based certification for teachers and administrators will become common.

	PROBABILITY OF OCCURRENCE				POTENTIAL FOR IMPACT ON SECONDARY SCHOOLS			
Yrs.	Doubtful	Possible	Likely	Certain	None	Marginal	Moderate	Strong
3-5	33	49	18	0	18	33	44	5
10	3	46	46	5	0	27	49	24

V. Institutional Factors *(continued)*

12. "Total experience" learning situations (i.e., survival trips, science camps, live-in museums) during the school year will become common.

Yrs.	PROBABILITY OF OCCURRENCE				POTENTIAL FOR IMPACT ON SECONDARY SCHOOLS			
	Doubtful	Possible	Likely	Certain	None	Marginal	Moderate	Strong
3-5	32	54	14	0	6	55	33	6
10	10	52	33	5	5	32	55	8

13. Student interscholastic athletics will be replaced by club teams sponsored by community groups.

Yrs.	PROBABILITY OF OCCURRENCE				POTENTIAL FOR IMPACT ON SECONDARY SCHOOLS			
	Doubtful	Possible	Likely	Certain	None	Marginal	Moderate	Strong
3-5	84	14	2	0	30	25	28	17
10	47	45	8	0	19	22	32	27

VI. Other Important Forces and Conditions

1. *(Please describe.)* _____
   _____
   _____

2. *(Please describe.)* _____
   _____
   _____

3. *(Please describe.)* _____
   _____
   _____

Appendix B

FUTURE FORCES AND CONDITIONS AFFECTING SECONDARY EDUCATION

I. Political and Legal Factors

National Political Leaders
(All figures are percentages)

1. A Department of Education will be established with a cabinet-level secretary.

Yrs.	PROBABILITY OF OCCURRENCE				POTENTIAL FOR IMPACT ON SECONDARY SCHOOLS			
	Doubtful	Possible	Likely	Certain	None	Marginal	Moderate	Strong
3-5	0	0	62	38	8	17	58	17
10	17	0	33	50	0	29	42	29

2. Federal control of secondary education (i.e., categorical aid programs, civil rights actions, reports on attendance and meals, Title IX, etc.) will grow.

Yrs.	PROBABILITY OF OCCURRENCE				POTENTIAL FOR IMPACT ON SECONDARY SCHOOLS			
	Doubtful	Possible	Likely	Certain	None	Marginal	Moderate	Strong
3-5	33	17	42	8	0	17	33	50
10	25	25	25	25	0	12	25	63

3. Desegregation efforts will be expanded in most metropolitan areas.

Yrs.	PROBABILITY OF OCCURRENCE				POTENTIAL FOR IMPACT ON SECONDARY SCHOOLS			
	Doubtful	Possible	Likely	Certain	None	Marginal	Moderate	Strong
3-5	15	46	31	8	0	31	31	38
10	14	29	57	0	0	14	57	29

4. Affirmative action programs will remain a central factor in job placement and college admissions.

Yrs.	PROBABILITY OF OCCURRENCE				POTENTIAL FOR IMPACT ON SECONDARY SCHOOLS			
	Doubtful	Possible	Likely	Certain	None	Marginal	Moderate	Strong
3-5	8	15	54	23	0	46	46	8
10	0	29	71	0	0	29	57	14

5. The courts will assert further the rights of children and youth.

Yrs.	PROBABILITY OF OCCURRENCE				POTENTIAL FOR IMPACT ON SECONDARY SCHOOLS			
	Doubtful	Possible	Likely	Certain	None	Marginal	Moderate	Strong
3-5	0	33	50	17	0	25	42	33
10	0	50	25	25	0	0	50	50

6. Organized teacher associations will become more powerful at the state and national levels.

Yrs.	PROBABILITY OF OCCURRENCE				POTENTIAL FOR IMPACT ON SECONDARY SCHOOLS			
	Doubtful	Possible	Likely	Certain	None	Marginal	Moderate	Strong
3-5	15	8	62	15	8	8	38	46
10	0	29	42	29	0	14	29	57

7. States will limit or eliminate the current education requirements for certification of teachers and school administrators.

Yrs.	PROBABILITY OF OCCURRENCE				POTENTIAL FOR IMPACT ON SECONDARY SCHOOLS			
	Doubtful	Possible	Likely	Certain	None	Marginal	Moderate	Strong
3-5	92	8	0	0	30	10	30	30
10	75	25	0	0	0	25	25	50

8. The age for compulsory education will be lowered in most states.

Yrs.	PROBABILITY OF OCCURRENCE				POTENTIAL FOR IMPACT ON SECONDARY SCHOOLS			
	Doubtful	Possible	Likely	Certain	None	Marginal	Moderate	Strong
3-5	75	25	0	0	11	22	22	45
10	63	37	0	0	12	12	12	64

9. Schools will be held accountable for specific, measurable results.

Yrs.	PROBABILITY OF OCCURRENCE				POTENTIAL FOR IMPACT ON SECONDARY SCHOOLS			
	Doubtful	Possible	Likely	Certain	None	Marginal	Moderate	Strong
3-5	0	15	70	15	0	0	33	67
10	0	0	71	29	0	0	0	100

10. Schools will lose "educational malpractice" litigation for awarding diplomas to students with insufficient skills.

Yrs.	PROBABILITY OF OCCURRENCE				POTENTIAL FOR IMPACT ON SECONDARY SCHOOLS			
	Doubtful	Possible	Likely	Certain	None	Marginal	Moderate	Strong
3-5	31	54	15	0	0	10	30	60
10	57	29	14	0	0	12	38	50

11. Legislation will be enacted to curtail collective bargaining rights for public school teachers.

Yrs.	PROBABILITY OF OCCURRENCE				POTENTIAL FOR IMPACT ON SECONDARY SCHOOLS			
	Doubtful	Possible	Likely	Certain	None	Marginal	Moderate	Strong
3-5	58	42	0	0	20	20	20	40
10	12	88	0	0	0	25	25	50

II. Economic Factors

1. Difficulties in the national economy will force schools to initiate additional budget cuts.

Yrs.	PROBABILITY OF OCCURRENCE				POTENTIAL FOR IMPACT ON SECONDARY SCHOOLS			
	Doubtful	Possible	Likely	Certain	None	Marginal	Moderate	Strong
3-5	33	25	9	33	10	0	40	50
10	12	12	51	25	0	0	37	63

2. Resistance will increase to the heavy use of property taxes to support local government, including schools.

Yrs.	PROBABILITY OF OCCURRENCE				POTENTIAL FOR IMPACT ON SECONDARY SCHOOLS			
	Doubtful	Possible	Likely	Certain	None	Marginal	Moderate	Strong
3-5	0	24	38	38	0	17	33	50
10	0	14	29	57	0	0	29	71

3. Income taxes and sales taxes will replace property taxes as the main source of school revenue.

Yrs.	PROBABILITY OF OCCURRENCE				POTENTIAL FOR IMPACT ON SECONDARY SCHOOLS			
	Doubtful	Possible	Likely	Certain	None	Marginal	Moderate	Strong
3-5	8	30	54	8	8	25	42	25
10	0	57	43	0	0	14	43	43

4. Financial support will be provided for private schools through tuition tax credits or by direct funding from tax revenues.

Yrs.	PROBABILITY OF OCCURRENCE				POTENTIAL FOR IMPACT ON SECONDARY SCHOOLS			
	Doubtful	Possible	Likely	Certain	None	Marginal	Moderate	Strong
3-5	23	62	15	0	8	8	17	67
10	0	43	57	0	0	14	14	72

5. Supplementary funding for special students (mentally handicapped, emotionally disturbed, etc.) will be cut back.

Yrs.	PROBABILITY OF OCCURRENCE				POTENTIAL FOR IMPACT ON SECONDARY SCHOOLS			
	Doubtful	Possible	Likely	Certain	None	Marginal	Moderate	Strong
3-5	85	15	0	0	10	30	40	20
10	29	71	0	0	0	29	57	14

6. Steps will be taken by federal and/or state governments to end school closures due to underfunding.

Yrs.	PROBABILITY OF OCCURRENCE				POTENTIAL FOR IMPACT ON SECONDARY SCHOOLS			
	Doubtful	Possible	Likely	Certain	None	Marginal	Moderate	Strong
3-5	9	27	46	18	0	18	27	55
10	12	25	51	12	0	14	14	72

7. Parents will be expected to purchase books and school supplies in the future.

Yrs.	PROBABILITY OF OCCURRENCE				POTENTIAL FOR IMPACT ON SECONDARY SCHOOLS			
	Doubtful	Possible	Likely	Certain	None	Marginal	Moderate	Strong
3-5	36	55	9	0	0	60	30	10
10	45	22	33	0	0	76	12	12

III. Social Factors

1. Society will become "deschooled" with most students learning in community settings.

Yrs.	PROBABILITY OF OCCURRENCE				POTENTIAL FOR IMPACT ON SECONDARY SCHOOLS			
	Doubtful	Possible	Likely	Certain	None	Marginal	Moderate	Strong
3-5	100	0	0	0	22	11	0	67
10	63	37	0	0	0	14	14	72

2. Concern for "quality-of-life" and "small-is-necessary" will foster major changes in the school's curriculum.

Yrs.	PROBABILITY OF OCCURRENCE				POTENTIAL FOR IMPACT ON SECONDARY SCHOOLS			
	Doubtful	Possible	Likely	Certain	None	Marginal	Moderate	Strong
3-5	15	62	23	0	0	22	78	0
10	0	25	63	12	0	29	71	0

3. Full employment and/or national service programs will be developed for youth.

Yrs.	PROBABILITY OF OCCURRENCE				POTENTIAL FOR IMPACT ON SECONDARY SCHOOLS			
	Doubtful	Possible	Likely	Certain	None	Marginal	Moderate	Strong
3-5	23	46	31	0	10	20	40	30
10	0	57	43	0	0	29	57	14

4. Business, industry, and labor will assume responsibilities for educating significant numbers of adolescents aged 16-18.

Yrs.	PROBABILITY OF OCCURRENCE				POTENTIAL FOR IMPACT ON SECONDARY SCHOOLS			
	Doubtful	Possible	Likely	Certain	None	Marginal	Moderate	Strong
3-5	50	40	10	0	0	37	26	37
10	20	40	40	0	11	11	56	22

III. Social Factors *(continued)*

5. Parents and citizens will expect to participate in establishing objectives and priorities for schools.

	PROBABILITY OF OCCURRENCE				POTENTIAL FOR IMPACT ON SECONDARY SCHOOLS			
Yrs.	Doubtful	Possible	Likely	Certain	None	Marginal	Moderate	Strong
3-5	2	8	67	25	0	17	59	33
10	0	0	63	37	0	14	57	29

6. "Social indicators" such as increase in crime, family breakdown, drug usage, etc. will result in additional new programs for schools.

	PROBABILITY OF OCCURRENCE				POTENTIAL FOR IMPACT ON SECONDARY SCHOOLS			
Yrs.	Doubtful	Possible	Likely	Certain	None	Marginal	Moderate	Strong
3-5	15	31	31	23	10	20	50	20
10	0	42	29	29	0	0	86	14

7. Social service functions such as serving breakfasts, providing psychological services, furnishing jobs, etc. will be assumed increasingly by nonschool agencies.

	PROBABILITY OF OCCURRENCE				POTENTIAL FOR IMPACT ON SECONDARY SCHOOLS			
Yrs.	Doubtful	Possible	Likely	Certain	None	Marginal	Moderate	Strong
3-5	18	73	9	0	10	40	30	20
10	12	44	44	0	0	25	63	12

8. Moral education or values education will become more common in high schools.

	PROBABILITY OF OCCURRENCE				POTENTIAL FOR IMPACT ON SECONDARY SCHOOLS			
Yrs.	Doubtful	Possible	Likely	Certain	None	Marginal	Moderate	Strong
3-5	27	55	9	9	10	30	50	10
10	22	56	11	11	12	25	51	12

9. Parents and society will grant youth aged 14-18 additional freedom in the future.

	PROBABILITY OF OCCURRENCE				POTENTIAL FOR IMPACT ON SECONDARY SCHOOLS			
Yrs.	Doubtful	Possible	Likely	Certain	None	Marginal	Moderate	Strong
3-5	32	39	15	7	0	22	33	45
10	25	50	25	0	0	29	29	42

IV. Technological Factors

1. Mini-computers, video-discs, and other technology will be widely used in schools.

	PROBABILITY OF OCCURRENCE				POTENTIAL FOR IMPACT ON SECONDARY SCHOOLS			
Yrs.	Doubtful	Possible	Likely	Certain	None	Marginal	Moderate	Strong
3-5	0	10	45	45	0	0	64	36
10	0	22	22	56	0	12	63	25

2. Much schooling will take place in the home through video and other new technologies.

	PROBABILITY OF OCCURRENCE				POTENTIAL FOR IMPACT ON SECONDARY SCHOOLS			
Yrs.	Doubtful	Possible	Likely	Certain	None	Marginal	Moderate	Strong
3-5	36	46	18	0	11	11	33	45
10	22	45	33	0	0	14	29	57

3. Drugs to control antisocial behavior and to improve mental performance will become common.

	PROBABILITY OF OCCURRENCE				POTENTIAL FOR IMPACT ON SECONDARY SCHOOLS			
Yrs.	Doubtful	Possible	Likely	Certain	None	Marginal	Moderate	Strong
3-5	84	8	8	0	12	12	25	51
10	25	50	25	0	0	0	33	67

4. Computer-assisted instruction will become common in schools.

	PROBABILITY OF OCCURRENCE				POTENTIAL FOR IMPACT ON SECONDARY SCHOOLS			
Yrs.	Doubtful	Possible	Likely	Certain	None	Marginal	Moderate	Strong
3-5	0	27	46	27	0	0	64	36
10	0	22	22	56	0	0	75	25

5. Instruction in oral and video-based communication will largely replace instruction about writing in secondary schools.

	PROBABILITY OF OCCURRENCE				POTENTIAL FOR IMPACT ON SECONDARY SCHOOLS			
Yrs.	Doubtful	Possible	Likely	Certain	None	Marginal	Moderate	Strong
3-5	60	40	0	0	0	12	38	50
10	44	44	12	0	0	12	38	50

V. Institutional Factors

1. Programs for adults in secondary schools will grow significantly.

PROBABILITY OF OCCURRENCE					POTENTIAL FOR IMPACT ON SECONDARY SCHOOLS			
Yrs.	Doubtful	Possible	Likely	Certain	None	Marginal	Moderate	Strong
3-5	0	9	64	27	0	30	30	40
10	0	0	33	67	0	11	33	56

2. Schools will become more "basic," cutting back on individual options and alternatives.

PROBABILITY OF OCCURRENCE					POTENTIAL FOR IMPACT ON SECONDARY SCHOOLS			
Yrs.	Doubtful	Possible	Likely	Certain	None	Marginal	Moderate	Strong
3-5	9	18	64	9	9	0	73	18
10	22	34	22	22	0	13	62	25

3. Federal funds will be distributed to support "parenting education."

PROBABILITY OF OCCURRENCE					POTENTIAL FOR IMPACT ON SECONDARY SCHOOLS			
Yrs.	Doubtful	Possible	Likely	Certain	None	Marginal	Moderate	Strong
3-5	0	100	0	0	0	67	33	0
10	22	45	33	0	12	50	38	0

4. Test scores will continue to drop.

PROBABILITY OF OCCURRENCE					POTENTIAL FOR IMPACT ON SECONDARY SCHOOLS			
Yrs.	Doubtful	Possible	Likely	Certain	None	Marginal	Moderate	Strong
3-5	31	46	23	0	15	7	39	39
10	66	17	17	0	0	0	67	33

5. The senior year of high school will disappear.

PROBABILITY OF OCCURRENCE					POTENTIAL FOR IMPACT ON SECONDARY SCHOOLS			
Yrs.	Doubtful	Possible	Likely	Certain	None	Marginal	Moderate	Strong
3-5	100	0	0	0	25	0	25	50
10	76	12	12	0	12	0	38	50

6. Private secondary schools will maintain or increase their enrollment as public school enrollment drops.

PROBABILITY OF OCCURRENCE					POTENTIAL FOR IMPACT ON SECONDARY SCHOOLS			
Yrs.	Doubtful	Possible	Likely	Certain	None	Marginal	Moderate	Strong
3-5	27	37	18	18	20	20	20	40
10	50	25	0	25	13	29	29	29

7. National standards for the high school diploma will be established.

PROBABILITY OF OCCURRENCE					POTENTIAL FOR IMPACT ON SECONDARY SCHOOLS			
Yrs.	Doubtful	Possible	Likely	Certain	None	Marginal	Moderate	Strong
3-5	60	20	20	0	30	0	30	40
10	19	63	9	9	10	10	40	40

8. The diploma will be established as a certificate of guarantee of basic skills.

PROBABILITY OF OCCURRENCE					POTENTIAL FOR IMPACT ON SECONDARY SCHOOLS			
Yrs.	Doubtful	Possible	Likely	Certain	None	Marginal	Moderate	Strong
3-5	36	28	36	0	0	18	46	36
10	10	70	10	10	0	11	56	33

9. Early graduation and other forms of early school leaving will diminish.

PROBABILITY OF OCCURRENCE					POTENTIAL FOR IMPACT ON SECONDARY SCHOOLS			
Yrs.	Doubtful	Possible	Likely	Certain	None	Marginal	Moderate	Strong
3-5	60	30	10	0	11	33	33	23
10	63	25	12	0	29	29	13	29

10. Teacher tenure will be severely curtailed or abolished in many states.

PROBABILITY OF OCCURRENCE					POTENTIAL FOR IMPACT ON SECONDARY SCHOOLS			
Yrs.	Doubtful	Possible	Likely	Certain	None	Marginal	Moderate	Strong
3-5	60	40	0	0	0	50	40	10
10	30	60	0	10	0	12	76	12

11. Competency-based certification for teachers and administrators will become common.

PROBABILITY OF OCCURRENCE					POTENTIAL FOR IMPACT ON SECONDARY SCHOOLS			
Yrs.	Doubtful	Possible	Likely	Certain	None	Marginal	Moderate	Strong
3-5	27	46	27	0	0	9	64	27
10	23	33	33	11	0	0	88	12

V. Institutional Factors *(continued)*

12. "Total experience" learning situations (i.e., survival trips, science camps, live-in museums) during the school year will become common.

	PROBABILITY OF OCCURRENCE				POTENTIAL FOR IMPACT ON SECONDARY SCHOOLS			
Yrs.	Doubtful	Possible	Likely	Certain	None	Marginal	Moderate	Strong
3-5	25	58	17	0	0	25	50	25
10	0	67	33	0	0	45	33	22

13. Student interscholastic athletics will be replaced by club teams sponsored by community groups.

	PROBABILITY OF OCCURRENCE				POTENTIAL FOR IMPACT ON SECONDARY SCHOOLS			
Yrs.	Doubtful	Possible	Likely	Certain	None	Marginal	Moderate	Strong
3-5	100	0	0	0	22	45	22	11
10	40	50	10	0	0	67	11	22

VI. Other Important Forces and Conditions

1. *(Please describe.)* _____

_____

_____

2. *(Please describe.)* _____

_____

_____

3. *(Please describe.)* _____

_____

_____

74

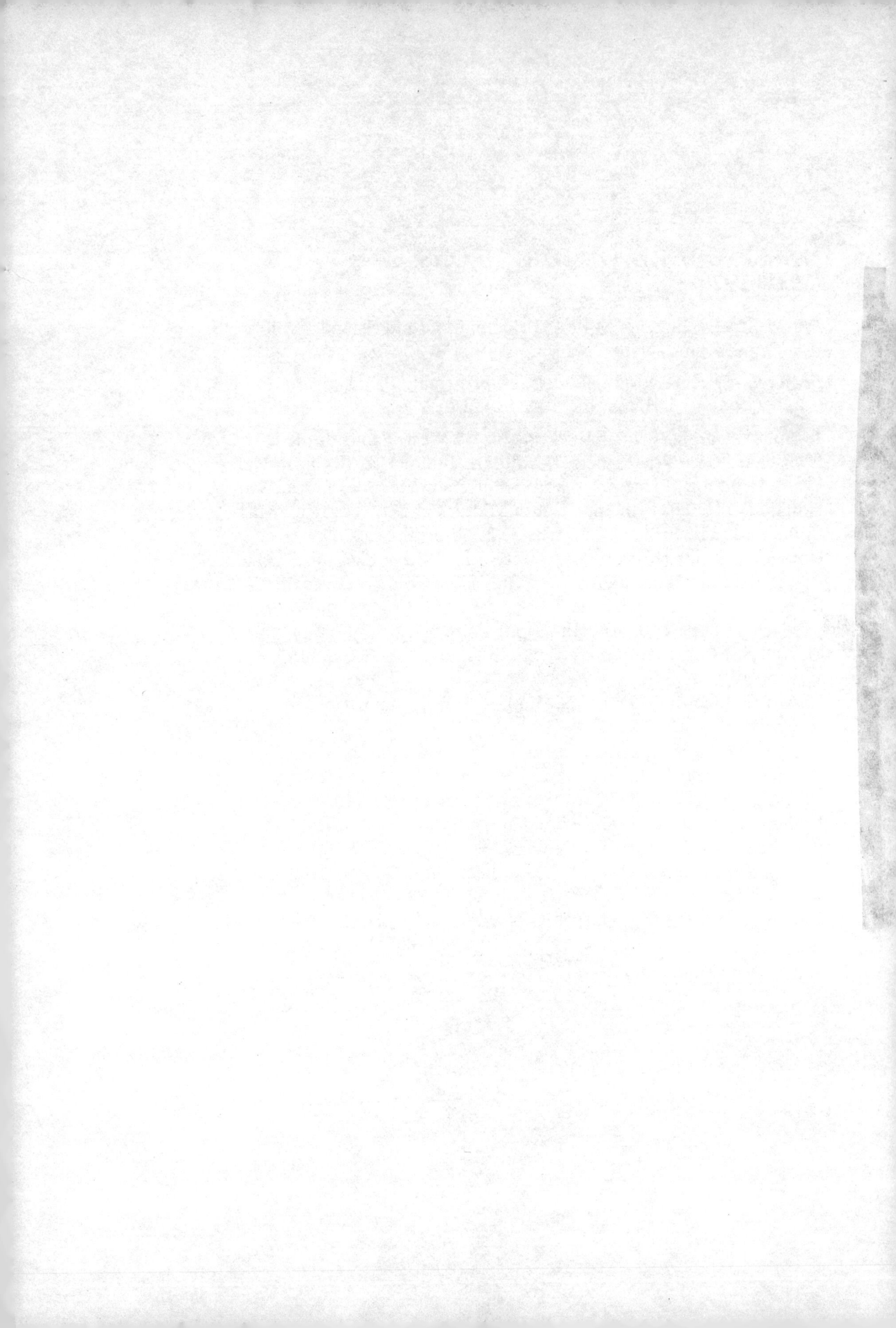